Ian Crofton now lives in London, but was born and raised in Edinburgh. He has written many works of popular history, including *History without the Boring Bits* (now published in many different languages around the world, from Japanese to Estonian) and *A Curious History of Food and Drink*. For Birlinn he has also written *A Dictionary of Scottish Phrase and Fable*. In 2013 he made a journey on foot along the Anglo-Scottish frontier, and the resulting book, *Walking the Border*, was selected by the *Daily Telegraph* as one of its travel books of 2014.

Scottish
HISTORY
without the
Boring Bits

———

a CHRONICLE *of*
the *CURIOUS*,
the ECCENTRIC,
the *ATROCIOUS*
and
the UNLIKELY

———

Ian Crofton

BIRLINN

First published in
Great Britain in 2015 by
Birlinn Ltd
West Newington House
10 Newington Road
Edinburgh
EH9 1QS

www.birlinn.co.uk

ISBN: 978 1 78027 265 8

British Library Cataloguing-in-Publication Data
A catalogue record for this book is available
from the British Library

Designed and typeset by
Mark Blackadder

Printed and bound by Grafica Veneta
www.graficaveneta.com

CONTENTS

INTRODUCTION

As will swiftly become apparent, the present volume differs from most serious works of historical scholarship in a number of respects. Not the least of these is the fact that only a certain proportion of the events mentioned herein actually took place. The same might be said of its *dramatis personae*: not absolutely all of them did, in reality, breathe the air of Scotland (certainly not the monsters and mermaids, demons, changelings and familiars). I suspect few modern historians accept that St Serf did in reality hear the bleating of a stolen sheep from within the stomach of the suspected thief. Or that poor Bessie Dunlop, burnt as a witch, consorted with the Good Folk of Elfhame. Or that on 23 September 1954 a vampire with iron teeth stalked Glasgow's Southern Necropolis.

Even if many of the events I describe *did* in fact take place, that does not necessarily mean they are historically significant. Significance is not the purpose of this book. Although many of the people and events herein are not important to our understanding of history, they may tell us something else, about the stories we tell ourselves about the past. Some such tales – Bruce and the Spider, Sawney Bean, Rob Roy – are so well known I thought it pointless to rehearse them again here. I have instead concentrated on digging up obscure little nuggets that throw some kind of curious sideways light on the nature and spirit of Scotland.

It may be that the present selection says more about the author than anything else. I have a tendency to suspect all those in authority of being rogues and hypocrites, and an associated penchant for pricking pomposity. I celebrate the bawdy and the subversive, the eccentric and the different, the put-upon and the misunderstood. I know I am not the only Scot to hold such attitudes, attitudes that run like a strong, pulsing vein through our history and culture. A hefty dose of snook-cocking lends vigour to our body politic, which might otherwise putrefy into a carcass reeking of piety, power lust, slack-jawed credulity and tut-tutting self-righteousness.

If all that sounds depressingly serious, I don't think that being depressingly serious is a thing this book can be accused of. I can only hope that the reader agrees.

Ian Crofton
February 2015

The
DARK *and*
MIDDLE
Ages

3948 BC
SCOTS EXPELLED FROM PARADISE

According to Sir Thomas Urquhart of Cromarty, the year 3948 BC was the date that God created 'of red earth' Urquhart's own ancestor Adam, by whom he claimed to be descended 143rd 'by line', and 153rd 'by succession'. Urquhart published his conclusions in 1652 in his *Panto-chronachanon*, subtitled *A Peculiar Promptuary of Time*. He initially follows the Old Testament genealogies (Enoch, Methuselah, Noah, Japhet, etc.), but by the late 3rd millennium BC wanders off into mythologies of his own creation. The year 2139 BC, he states, was the date of birth of Esormon, sovereign prince of Achaia: 'For his fortune in the wars, and affability in conversation, his subjects and familiars surnamed him OUROCHARTOS, that is to say, *fortunate and well beloved*. After which time, his posterity ever since hath acknowledged him the father of all that carry the name of URQUHART.' Fortune in war and affability in conversation were qualities that Sir Thomas prized above all in himself: a dashing Cavalier, he fought for the Royalist side in the Wars of the Three Kingdoms, and published a succession of mock-scholarly works in which he floated a range of improbable notions, unfeasible inventions and even a new universal language (see 1653).

circa who knows when? BC
THE ORIGINS OF THE SCOTS IN SCYTHIA
(OR GREECE, OR EGYPT, OR SPAIN)

According to some of the medieval chroniclers, the Scots had their origins in Scythia, the area of steppes north of the Black Sea whose nomadic, pastoral inhabitants were described by the ancient Greeks. The supposed peregrinations of these proto-Scots is described in the Declaration of Arbroath (1320):

> From the chronicles and books of the ancients we find that among other famous nations our own, the Scots, have been graced with widespread renown. They journeyed from Greater Scythia by way of the Tyrrhenian Sea and the Pillars

of Hercules, and dwelt for a long course of time in Spain among the most savage tribes, but nowhere could they be subdued by any race, however barbarous. Thence they came, twelve hundred years after the people of Israel crossed the Red Sea, to their home in the west where they still live today.

The earliest version of the story appears to be an 11th-century Irish manuscript, which relates that the Gaels were descended from the Scythian prince Fénius Farsaid, one of the 72 princes who supposedly had a hand in the construction of the Tower of Babel. Fénius's son Nél married an Egyptian princess called Scota (hence 'Scotia', 'Scotland', etc.), and they begot Goídel Glas (Latinised as Gathelus), who was credited with creating the Gaelic language when God 'confounded the language of all the Earth'. In the version concocted by the Scottish chronicler John of Fordun in the 14th century, Goídel Glas becomes Gaythelos, a Greek prince who was exiled to Egypt, where he married the pharaoh's daughter, Scota. They appear to have left Egypt for Spain at the time of the biblical plagues, and the subsequent death of the pharaoh and his army pursuing Moses and the Israelites across the Red Sea. Neither of these accounts is now generally accepted by historians.

AD 26

PONTIUS PILATE WAS A PERTHSHIRE LAD

Pontius Pilate became prefect of the Roman province of Judaea. There is a longstanding tradition that he was born in Fortingall in Perthshire, his father supposedly having been a Roman ambassador and his mother a local Menzies or a MacLaren. Whatever the truth of this, Fortingall has a more secure claim to fame in the form of the ancient Fortingall Yew, thought to be between 3,000 and 5,000 years old.

circa 380
CANNIBALISTIC CALEDONIANS

St Jerome, visiting Gaul, 'learned that the Attacotti, the people of the country now called Scotland, when hunting in the woods, preferred the shepherd to his flocks, and chose only the most fleshy and delicate parts for eating'.

548
ST COLUMBA BURIES FELLOW SAINT ALIVE

Death of St Oran on Iona. Legend has it that as his companion St Columba tried to build a chapel on the island, every night the demons of the place demolished it. In order to propitiate the *genus loci*, St Oran agreed to be buried alive. After three days Columba ordered that his friend be dug up. To the horror of all present, Oran 'declared that there was neither a God, a judgement nor a future state'. Such views being entirely unacceptable, Columba ordered that Oran be forthwith buried alive for a second time, this time on a permanent basis.

circa 561
WINNING BY A FINGER

The Irish missionaries St Moluag and St Mulhac eyed up the island of Lismore north of Oban with the idea of founding a monastery there. Legend recounts how the two rivals agreed to a rowing race across Loch Linnhe to the island, with the winner becoming the founder of the monastery. As his rival pulled ahead towards the end of the race, St Moluag resorted to a desperate measure: he cut off one of his own fingers and flung it to the shore, so winning the race. He went on to establish his monastery at the place called Kilmoluaig, meaning 'Moluag's church'.

583

THE SILENCE OF THE RAMS

Death of St Serf. Among his many miracles, the following is probably the most remarkable. The saint had a favourite ram, which would follow him wherever he went. But one day the ram was stolen. Suspicion fell upon a certain man, who was brought before the saint. The man flatly denied he had anything to do with the ram's disappearance. But then a bleating was heard coming from the man's stomach. The ram – which he had killed, cooked and devoured – thus confirmed the man's guilt.

617

EXTERMINATIONS ON EIGG

St Donan, who had established a monastery on the island of Eigg, was burnt alive along with 150 of his monks by a band of wild warrior women under the command of a pagan Pictish queen. A 17th-century Irish chronicler gives an alternative account of St Donan's demise:

> And there came robbers of the sea on a certain time to the island when he was celebrating mass. He requested of them not to kill him until he should have the mass said, and they gave him this respite; and he was afterwards beheaded and fifty-two of his monks along with him.

Many years later, in 1577, the island witnessed another massacre, inflicted by a raiding party of MacLeods from Skye on the native MacDonalds. On a previous visit, a band of MacLeods, intent on ravishing the maidenhood of Eigg, had been castrated by the outraged MacDonalds; alternatively, they had been bound hand and foot and set adrift, but were rescued by their fellow clansmen. The MacLeods returned in force, obliging the MacDonalds to hide in a cave. The raiders discovered them, lit a fire at the entrance and wafted the smoke into the dark interior, where 200 of the fugitives were asphyxiated. Visiting the 'Massacre Cave' in 1814, Sir Walter Scott reported that he found 'numerous specimens of mortality'. The remains remained unburied for some decades after his visit.

The vendetta was by no means at an end. The year after the massacre at the cave, a band of MacDonalds landed on Skye at Trumpan, herded the local MacLeods into a church, barred the door, and set it alight. Only one person escaped alive, a young girl, who fled to Dunvegan. A strong force of MacLeods went forth and slaughtered the invaders, lined up their bodies under a turf wall and toppled the wall over to bury them.

circa 650
THE SAINT WHO NEARLY WASN'T

Loth or Lleuddun, Chief of the Votadani and King of the Lothians, was furious when he discovered his daughter Teneu was pregnant. In his wrath he ordered that she be thrown down the cliffs on the south side of Traprain Law, former capital of the Votadani. As she fell, Teneu prayed for forgiveness, and came to earth unharmed. Loth, however, concluded from this that she was a witch, and had her cast into the sea near the Isle of May. Again she survived, this time by clinging onto the rock still known as Maiden Hair Rock. From here she was swept up the Firth of Forth, eventually coming ashore at Culross, where she gave birth to the boy who was to become St Kentigern (or Mungo), who built the first church in what is now Glasgow.

687
COFFIN USED TO WATER COWS

(20 March) Death of St Cuthbert. Many stories are told about the fate of his body after his death. One legend recounts how it was enclosed in a stone coffin at Melrose, from where it sailed down the Tweed until coming ashore at the mouth of the River Till (where St Cuthbert's Chapel now stands). Cuthbert's body was then taken on to Durham, but the stone coffin stayed by the chapel for some centuries. When a local farmer began to use the coffin to water his cattle, the saint's angry spirit smashed it to pieces. (This last part of the story appears to have been confected by the Revd Lambe, a vicar of Norham.)

circa 720

EYELESS IN ORKNEY

On a visit to Papa Westray in Orkney, King Nechtan of the Picts was smitten by the beautiful eyes of a local girl, one Triduana or Trollhaena. She, however, did not reciprocate his feelings, and rather than giving him her body, she plucked out her eyes and gave him those instead. Triduana subsequently became abbess of a convent at Restalrig (now part of Edinburgh), and was later canonised as St Tredwell. A chapel dedicated to her still stands on Papa Westray, beside St Tredwell's Loch, and was long a destination for those suffering from eye problems.

ONE SAINTLY HAND IS WORTH A HUNDRED CANDLES

Also around this time flourished St Fillan, a saint of Irish origin who was abbot at Pittenweem in Fife before retiring as a hermit to Glendochart in Perthshire. He was buried at Strathfillan. It was said that he was enabled to continue transcribing the Scriptures after dark owing to the miraculous light-emitting power of his left hand, thus saving his abbey a fortune in candles. So treasured was this arm of St Fillan that Robert the Bruce carried it into battle at Bannockburn, and to this relic he attributed his victory. As late as the 19th century, those suffering from mental illness were dipped in a pool at Strathfillan, and then tied up in a corner of the ruined chapel overnight. If their bonds had worked lose by the morning, then the saint had restored them to sanity.

809

THE LOVE THAT DARE NOT SPEAK ITS NAME

Legend traces the Auld Alliance between Scotland and France to a treaty supposedly made this year between a Scots king called Achaius or Eochaid and the Emperor Charlemagne, by which the former agreed to help the latter in his fight against the Saxons. However, the first treaty between the two countries of which there is any evidence dates from 1295. Despite a number of vicissitudes, the spirit of amity between the two nations has persisted into the present century. In 2009, for example, President Nicolas Sarkozy of France addressed Prime Minister Gordon Brown with the following words:

You know, Gordon, I should not like you. You are Scottish, we have nothing in common and you are an economist. But somehow, Gordon, I love you. But not in a sexual way.

995
KING KILLED BY MURDEROUS STATUE

Finella, daughter of Cuncar, Mormaer of Angus, sought revenge on King Kenneth II, whom she held responsible for the death of her son. According to the 14th-century chronicler John of Fordun, she lured the king to a cottage in Fettercairn, where she showed him the statue of a boy, and urged him to touch the boy's head. When he did so, the movement triggered a number of hidden crossbows, which fired their bolts into Kenneth's body with fatal effect. Finella fled to the coast near St Cyrus, where she was cornered by Kenneth's men in a steep valley with a waterfall. Rather than fall into their hands, she threw herself over the waterfall to her death. To this day, the place is known as 'Den Finella' (grid reference NO 765 6745).

1010
THREE BLOODY STROKES ON A COAT OF ARMS

According to legend, at the Battle of Barry in Angus an ancestor of the Keith family (later Earls Marischal) killed the Viking leader, Camus. To Keith's anger, another Scottish warrior claimed that he had killed Camus. To resolve this, the king, Malcolm II, decreed that the two men should enter single combat. Keith was victorious, and before his death his opponent confessed to his lie. Malcolm then dipped his fingers in the dead man's blood and drew three bloody strokes across Keith's shield – a device born on the arms of the family to this day.

1098
TURNING KINTYRE INTO AN ISLAND

Magnus Barefoot, King of Norway, mounted an onslaught on the west coast of Scotland. Desperate for peace, King Edgar of Scotland agreed to renounce all Scottish claims to the islands west of the mainland –

which were anyway already under Norwegian control. Magnus managed to extend his territory even further by having his ship dragged across the narrow isthmus at Tarbert, thus demonstrating (to his own satisfaction at least) that the peninsula of Kintyre, part of the mainland, was also an island.

circa 1117

PSALM-SINGING EARL HAS SKULL CLEFT

Death of Magnus Erlendsson, Earl of Orkney. He had failed to win popularity with his fellow Norsemen by refusing to fight during a raid on Anglesey, instead staying on board his ship singing psalms. Returning to Orkney, he ruled jointly with his cousin Haakon, but they later fell out. Magnus ended up the loser, and found himself Haakon's prisoner. Haakon ordered his standard bearer, Ofeigr, to put Magnus to death, but Ofeigr refused. So Haakon, in a fury, told his cook to dispatch Magnus with an axe blow to the head. Before this unpleasantness, Magnus is said to have prayed for his executioner (whoever it should turn out to be). The piety of his life, the manner of his death, and the subsequent miracles attributed to him earned Magnus a sainthood. In 1919, in St Magnus's Cathedral in Kirkwall, a cleft skull and some other bones were found within one of the pillars of the cathedral. These are generally believed to be genuine relics.

circa 1150

AN ARAB VIEW OF SCOTLAND:
RAIN, MISTS AND DARKNESS

The Arab geographer Muhammad al-Idrisi wrote that Scotland (or 'Squtlandiyah') 'is uninhabited and has neither town nor village'. Formerly there had been three towns, he said, but civil war had resulted in the deaths of nearly all the inhabitants. To the west of Scotland lay the Sea of Darkness, from whence

> there come continually mists and rain, and the sky is always overcast, particularly on the coast. The waters of this sea are covered with cloud and dark in colour. The waves are

enormous, and the sea is deep. Darkness reigns continually, and navigation is difficult. The winds are violent and towards the west its limits are unknown.

1153
'THORNI FUCKED, HELGI CARVED'

A party of Norsemen led by Earl Harald found themselves caught in a blizzard while making their way from Stromness to Firth, on Orkney Mainland. They took shelter by breaking in through the roof of Maes Howe, a chambered cairn that had been built some 4,000 years previously. The newcomers whiled away the time waiting for the weather to clear by scrawling runic graffiti on the walls. 'These runes were carved by the man most skilled in runes in the western ocean,' wrote one. 'Ingigerth is the most beautiful of all women,' wrote another, beside a drawing of a slavering dog. A third man simply wrote, 'Thorni fucked, Helgi carved.'

1219
EVIL SPIRITS REJOICE AT BROKEN FASTS

Foundation of Deer Abbey in Buchan. John of Fordun, the 14th-century chronicler, tells us that the first abbot, Robert, was renowned for his piety. On one particular meat-free fast day, after eating his mandatory fish, Robert became immersed in holy contemplation, when 'a figure of an Ethiopian, black as darkness, appeared to him, and then, with a loud laugh, vanished from his presence'. Robert suspected what was afoot, and summoned the cook before him. There was only one explanation, Robert told the cook. The man had served the fish not in butter, but in animal fat. Ashamed, the cook confessed that this had indeed been the case. 'How must evil spirits rejoice,' wrote Fordun, 'when monks, in disobedience to the rules of their order, eat flesh on days when it is prohibited.'

1222

BISHOP ROASTED IN BUTTER

Abbot Adam of Melrose, Bishop of Caithness since 1214, had become increasingly unpopular with the locals for the rigour with which he exacted his tithes, even going so far as to excommunicate several of them for failing to pay their allotted portion. Things became intolerable when he doubled the duty on the ownership of cows, a tax that was payable in butter. The people took their grievances to the Earl of Caithness, who appears to have been as irritated with the plaintiffs as he was with the man they were complaining about. 'The Devil take the bishop and his butter,' the Earl exclaimed. 'You may roast him if you please!' The plaintiffs took this as an order, and an angry mob set off to the Bishop's palace. The Bishop sent out a monk called Serlo to pacify them, but as soon as he appeared he was clubbed to the ground and then stamped to death. When the Bishop himself emerged to discuss an amicable settlement, the mob would have none on it. They seized the prelate, dragged him to his own kitchen, stoked up the fire, and there roasted him in a large quantity of the butter that he had gathered in tithes.

When news of this 'horrid deed' was brought to King Alexander II in Jedburgh, he immediately set out on the long journey north. When he arrived in Caithness, he ordered that the perpetrators should be hanged, and that those who were not hanged should have their hands and feet cut off. This proceeding was praised in a bull by Pope Clement IV.

1251

THE WEIGHT OF MAJESTY

The body of the sainted Queen Margaret, consort of Malcolm Canmore ('big head'), was removed from its burial place in Dunfermline and placed in a lavish shrine. In his *Historical Collections concerning the Scottish History preceding the death of King David I* (1705), Sir James Dalrymple tells us what happened next:

> While the monks were employed in this service, they
> approached the tomb of her husband Malcolm. The body [of

the queen] became, on a sudden, so heavy, that they were obliged to set it down. Still, as more hands were employed in raising it, the body became heavier. The spectators stood amazed; and the humble monks imputed this phenomenon to their own unworthiness, when a bystander cried out: 'The queen will not stir till equal honours are performed to her husband.' This having been done, the body of the queen was removed with ease. A more awkward miracle occurs not in legendary history.

1271

THE COUNTESS GETS HER MAN

Marjorie, Countess of Carrick, learnt of the death of her first husband, Adam of Kilconquhar, in the Eighth Crusade. The young man who brought her these tidings was Robert de Brus, Lord of Annandale. According to legend, Marjorie was so captivated by the young man that she kept him prisoner in Turnberry Castle until he agreed to marry her. Among their nine children was the future Robert I of Scotland – Robert the Bruce.

1285

SKELETON DANCES AT FEAST

King Alexander III married his second wife, Yolande de Dreux, in Jedburgh Abbey. At the subsequent feast, in the words of Sir James Dalrymple, 'a ghost, or something like a ghost, danced'. He continues:

> Boece expressely says that it was a skeleton. A foolish pleas-antry to frighten the court ladies, or a pious monastic fraud, to check the growth of promiscuous dancing, probably gave rise to this harlequin skeleton.

The apparition was remembered with a shudder when only a year later news spread that the king had met with a fatal accident, falling from his horse over a cliff while rushing to be reunited with his bride of one year.

1307
THE DOUGLAS LARDER

On Palm Sunday Sir James Douglas – aka the Black Douglas aka the Guid Schir James – recaptured his own Douglas Castle and beheaded the entire English garrison. Both heads and bodies were piled up on top of the castle's food stores in the cellar, and then the whole thing set alight. Douglas did not have enough men to hold the castle, so he withdrew, but not before dropping salt and dead horses into the wells. The incident became known as 'the Douglas Larder'.

1308
BURIED ALIVE?

Death of the philosopher John Duns Scotus, who was born in the Berwickshire town of Duns. It is possible that he was not in fact dead when he was buried, as, according to tradition, when his grave was later opened, he was found outside his coffin, his hands torn and bloody as if he had made some desperate effort to escape.

1313
CUNNING COWS

(19 February) The Black Douglas captured Roxburgh Castle from the English. Rather than risking a frontal assault, as the light faded he disguised his men as black cattle, and in this way they were able to creep close enough to the walls to put up their siege ladders without being detected.

1330
BOLD HEARTS AND BOILED CORPSES

After the death of Robert the Bruce in 1329, the Black Douglas set out to fulfil his promise to his king to take his heart on crusade to the Holy Land, in order to atone for Bruce's murder of the Red Comyn in church in 1306. Douglas's route took him to Spain, where he fought alongside Alfonso XI of Castile against the Moors of Granada. Finding himself surrounded and impossibly outnumbered, Douglas – at least according to legend – took the silver casket containing Bruce's heart from around his neck and flung it into the enemy host. With that he hurled himself forward to death and glory – and thereafter the Douglas motto became 'Doe or Die'. After the battle, the Moorish commander recovered his body and the casket, and returned them to Alfonso. Douglas's corpse was then boiled, the flesh buried in Spain and the bones taken back to Scotland, where they were buried in St Bride's Church, Douglas. Bruce's heart was interred in Melrose Abbey. Subsequently, the Douglas family arms incorporated a bloody heart.

1333
AN IRON LADY

An English army under Edward III laid siege to Berwick, which was defended by its governor, Sir Alexander Seton. Edward sent a message to Seton, telling him that if he did not surrender, his son Thomas, whom Edward held hostage, would be hanged. As the English built a scaffold before the walls of the town, Seton's resolve began to weaken. According to legend, he might have agreed to surrender had it not been for the intervention of his wife. 'We are young enough to have more children,' she supposedly told her husband, 'but if we surrender, we can never recover the loss of our honour.' So Seton held out against the English, even standing up on the town walls to witness his son being hanged. As for Lady Seton, she afterwards gave birth to two more sons.

That at least is the legend. In fact, the couple had already lost two sons, Alexander and William, fighting the English for David II. Seton himself died around 1348, all his sons having died before him.

1338
BLACK AGNES HOLDS THE FORT

Patrick, Earl of Dunbar, was elsewhere when his castle at Dunbar was placed under siege by an English army under William Montague, Earl of Salisbury. The command of the castle was thus left to his wife, Agnes Randolph, known as 'Black Agnes' because, according to the later chronicler Robert Lindsay of Pitscottie, she was 'blak skynnit'.

Pitscottie opined that she was 'of greater spirit than it became a woman to be', a somewhat grudging view in the light of the formidable defence she mounted against the enemy. When the English started to catapult rocks at the walls, the countess commanded her maids to sweep the battlements with brushes, as if the rocks were no more than flecks of dust. When the English brought up the Sow, a kind of siege tower, she remained defiant. 'Beware, Montagow,' she mocked, 'for farrow shall they sow.' With that she ordered her men to smash down the Sow with one of the catapulted rocks. 'Behold the litter of English pigs,' she shouted, as the English inside clambered out and fled for their lives. In exasperation, Salisbury decided to play what he thought was his trump card. He had as his captive Agnes's younger brother, the Earl of Moray, and now he brought him into view before the castle with a rope round his neck, telling Agnes that he would be hanged unless she surrendered. She simply told Salisbury to proceed with the execution, as then she'd inherit her brother's lands and title. In the end, Salisbury abandoned the siege. Her deeds were celebrated in a ballad, which has the English commander despair of ever besting his opponent:

> She kept a stir in tower and trench,
> That brawling, boisterous Scottish wench;
> Cam I early, cam I late,
> There was Agnes at the gate.

circa 1339
CHRISTIE-CLEEK THE CANNIBAL

After the armies of Edward III had laid waste some of the more fertile parts of the country, famine stalked the land. Rumours emerged that a butcher from Perth called Andrew Christie had fled to the southern foothills of the Grampians, and there resorted to desperate means to fill his belly. He would, it was said, use a crook to pull travellers from their horses, and then set about butchering, cooking and devouring them. This figure became known as Christie-Cleek (a *cleek* being a crook), and Christie-Cleek was long used as a bogeyman to frighten children into good behaviour.

1342
A HUMILIATING END

After his capture of Roxburgh Castle from the English, Sir Alexander Ramsay of Dalhousie was appointed as Constable of the castle and Sheriff of Teviotdale by David II. This was taken amiss by another great Border magnate, Sir William Douglas of Liddesdale, who had unsuccessfully tried to retake the castle, of which he had been Constable. Furious at what he saw as a threat to his own sphere of influence, Douglas seized Ramsay in Hawick, and imprisoned him in Hermitage Castle without food. Ramsay, it was said, managed to survive for 17 days on grains trickling through the floorboards from the granary above his cell, before finally succumbing to starvation.

1355
REVENGE IS A DISH BEST SERVED COLD

A French knight serving with the Scots at the Battle of Nisbet Moor near Duns took a cruel revenge for the death of his father, who had been killed by the English in France. He purchased the many common English soldiers who had been captured, led them away to a secluded place, and cut their heads off. The place became known as Slaughter Hill.

1356
EARL BEATEN ABOUT THE HEAD WITH BOOT

Among the Scots soldiers taken prisoner by the English at the Battle of Poitiers was Archibald the Grim, Earl of Douglas. From his splendid armour, the English quite rightly took him for a great lord, who would therefore command a huge ransom.

To avert this eventuality, one of Douglas's companions, Sir William Ramsay of Colluthy, looked the Earl straight in the eye and cried out, as if in a violent passion, 'You cursed damnable murderer, how comes it, in the name of mischief, *exparte diaboli*, that you are thus proudly decked in your master's armour? Come hither and pull off my boots.'

Taking up the game, Douglas approached Sir William, trembling and fearful, and pulled off one of his boots, which Sir William immediately used to beat him about the head.

The English intervened, saying that he should not beat a lord of so high a rank.

'What? He a lord?' exclaimed Sir William. 'He is a scullion, and a base knave, and, as I suppose, has killed his master. Go, you villain, to the field, search for the body of my cousin, your master. And when you have found it, come back, that at least I may give him a decent burial.'

Then, handing over a modest ransom of 40 shillings for the 'serving man', and roaring, 'Get you gone! Fly!', he delivered a parting kick to Douglas's backside. And so the Earl made good his escape.

'This story, as to some of its circumstances, may not seem altogether probable,' admits Alexander Hislop, who printed it in *The Book of Scottish Anecdote* (1888). 'Yet in the main it has the appearance of truth.' The story was also included in Sir Herbert Maxwell's *History of the House of Douglas* (1902).

1388

DEAD MAN WINS FIGHT

At the Battle of Otterburn, a Scots force under James, Earl of Douglas, defeated the English under Henry Percy (Shakespeare's Harry Hotspur). Douglas was fatally wounded in the fight, and as he slowly expired he ordered that he be hidden in a stand of bracken so that the enemy would not take heart from hearing of his death. Despite the loss of their leader, the Scots were victorious, and it was to the stand of bracken in which the dead Douglas lay that Hotspur acknowledged defeat – hence the celebrated verse in the ballad 'The Battle of Otter-bourne':

But I hae dream'd a dreary dream,
Beyond the Isle of Skye;
I saw a dead man win a fight,
And I think that man was I.

1390

AN EYE FOR AN EYE

On a diplomatic visit to the court of King Richard II in London, Sir David Lindsay (later 1st Earl of Crawford), had among his retinue Sir William Dalzell, a knight noted as much for his wit as for his wisdom. Among the English courtiers they encountered was Sir Piers Courtenay, famed both for his jousting skills and for the attention that he paid to his person. One day Courtenay appeared at the palace in a new mantle, embroidered with a falcon and the following rhyme:

> I bear a falcon, fairest of flight,
> Who so pinches at her, his death is dight,
> In graith.

The following day Dalzell turned up in an identical mantle, but bearing a magpie rather than a falcon and embroidered with a different motto:

> I bear a pie picking at a piece,
> Who so picks at her, I shall pick at his nese [nose],
> In faith.

Courtenay was mortified, and challenged Dalzell to joust with sharpened lances. Reckoning his chances of surviving were slim, Dalzell loosened the laces of his helmet, so that when Courtenay's lance struck his helmet it flew off, saving him from the shock of the blow. This happened again at the second joust, and at the third Courtenay lost a couple of teeth. He complained bitterly to the king, and Dalzell agreed to six more jousts, but this time with both parties putting down a deposit of £200, to be forfeited if either champion could be shown to possess an unfair advantage. Dalzell, who had lost an eye at the Battle of Otterburn two years previously, then demanded that Courtenay sacrifice one of his eyes, so that the two knights should enter the lists with equal optical powers. Courtenay refused, and angrily appealed to the king. But Richard ruled that Courtenay had forfeited his £200, which he handed over to Dalzell. The Scottish knight, he said, had surpassed the English knight in both valour and wit.

1398

ROSLIN MAN BEATS COLUMBUS TO NEW WORLD

Henry Sinclair of Roslin, Earl of Orkney, together with the brothers Nicolò and Antonio Zeno of Venice and 300 settlers, is said to have landed in Nova Scotia, nearly 100 years before Columbus reached the New World. This theory has drawn support from those of a Holy Blood and Holy Grail tendency, who link Sinclair to the Knights Templar and who have pointed out the supposed resemblance of carvings of plants in Roslin Chapel (built by Henry's grandson) to native North American plants. The more level-headed suggest these carvings are stylised depictions of wheat and strawberry plants. The story appears to have originated in a hoax perpetrated by the Zeno brothers, or possibly their descendant, another Nicolò Zeno, who published their letters in 1558. Supporters of the theory insist that the 'Prince Zichmni' in these letters, with whom the Zenos sail across the Atlantic, is Henry Sinclair. In 1996 the Prince Henry Sinclair Society erected a monument to their hero at Chedabucto Bay in Nova Scotia. But as *The Dictionary of Canadian Biography* says, 'the Zeno affair remains one of the most preposterous and at the same time one of the most successful fabrications in the history of exploration'.

1402

DUKE EATS HIS OWN FINGERS

King Robert III having been declared incapable of ruling the kingdom on account of the 'sickness of his person', the management of the kingdom was in the hands of his brother, the Duke of Albany. Eventually a power struggle arose between Albany and Robert's son, the Duke of Rothesay, culminating in late 1401 when Albany had Rothesay arrested and confined in his castle at Falkland, the accusation being that Rothesay had appropriated customs revenues from the burghs of the east coast. The historian Hector Boece (1465–1536) gives a more colourful reason for Rothesay's imprisonment, recounting that after his mother's death the young man had abandoned all 'virtews and honest occupatioun' and 'began to rage in all manner of insolence; and fulyeit [defiled] virginis, matronis, and nunnis, by his unbridillit lust'.

According to Boece, Robert III, disgusted by his son's behaviour, had written to Albany to ask him to 'intertene' Rothesay and teach the young man 'honest and civill maneris'.

Boece goes on to recount how Rothesay was kept in a tower at Falkland, without 'ony meit or drink'. His life was prolonged for some days when a certain woman, taking pity on the young Duke, trickled meal down to his place of confinement from the loft above. However, her ruse was discovered, and she was put to death. Another tender woman tried to feed him milk from her breast through 'ane lang reid', but was also found out, and 'wes slane with gret cruelte'. In despera tion, Boece continues, Rothesay resorted to eating not only 'the filth of the toure quhare he wes', but also his own fingers. Boece was elabo rating rumours that widely circulated at the time, but it is conceivable that Rothesay's death in late March 1402 was due to natural causes, possibly dysentery. This was certainly the view of the General Council that met to consider the matter in May 1402, concluding that Rothesay's death was caused 'by divine providence'.

1405
THE WOLF PLAYS CHESS WITH THE DEVIL

Death of Alexander Stewart, Earl of Buchan, known as the Wolf of Badenoch owing to his irregular conduct (his abandonment of his wife, his burning of Elgin Cathedral, his general taste for rapine and plunder). According to legend, Buchan was visited at Ruthven Castle just before his death by a tall stranger, dressed in black, who asked to play a game of chess with his host. Buchan agreed to the match. Eventually the stranger was heard to say 'Checkmate', upon which a terrible thunderstorm commenced, and continued through the night. In the morning Buchan's body was found dead, without a mark, although the nails in his boots had all been torn out. He was buried in Dunkeld Cathedral, where his sarcophagus, with his armoured effigy recumbent upon it, can still be seen.

circa 1430
A WOMAN CRUELLY SHOD

During the reign of James I, a poor woman in the Highlands was robbed of her two cattle by the chief of a band of caterans. She loudly declared that she would never again put on her shoes till she had carried her complaint to the king. 'Not so,' the chief sneered. 'I'll have you shod myself before you reach the court.' And he proceeded to nail two horseshoes to her naked feet, before pushing her on to the high road. A passing Samaritan found her crippled and bleeding, and took her in until her feet were mended. Then the woman continued on her way, eventually showing the king the horrible scars on her feet. James was outraged, and sent a writ out for the arrest of the robber-chief. The latter was soon seized and taken to Perth, where he was tried, paraded through the streets tied to a horse's tail, and hanged.

1437
KING STABBED IN PRIVY

The attempts by King James I to undermine the Perthshire power base of his uncle, Walter Stewart, Earl of Atholl, led to a deadly feud between the two, culminating in the death of both. Part of the problem seems to have been that a group of witches had told the Earl that he would one day wear the crown. This led Atholl in 1437 to hatch a plot against the king, in conspiracy with his grandson Robert Stewart and Sir Robert Graham. While James was staying at the Blackfriars Monastery in Perth, Graham and a small band of assassins made their entry. According to legend, someone had removed the bolts from the door of the royal chamber, and Catherine Douglas, one the queen's serving women, inserted her own arm to bar the door – forever after earning the nickname 'Kate Barlass'. To no avail: the assassins hurled themselves against the door, breaking Catherine's arm, and gaining entry. At this point the king attempted a subterranean escape, plunging down the privy. By an ironic stroke of fate, only three days earlier James had ordered that the exit of the privy on the outside of the building be stopped up, as he was annoyed that so many of his tennis balls ended up rolling down 'that foul hole'. So now the king was trapped, and the assassins quickly finished him off with their daggers.

Atholl's attempted coup received no support, and soon he and his co-conspirators were arrested and brought to trial. The verdict was predictable, but even by the standards of that era, Atholl's sentence was grisly. His execution was stretched out over three days. On the first day he was hoisted upside-down into the air by a rope attached to his ankles, then repeatedly dropped to the ground. On the second day he was put in a pillory and his head crowned with a red-hot iron band bearing the legend 'The King of Traitors', before being dragged through the streets on a hurdle. On the last day, 26 March 1437, while he was still conscious, his bowels were slowly pulled from his belly and burnt before his eyes; then, to make an end at last, his heart was ripped out and his head cut off. The mutilated body was quartered, the segments being displayed in Edinburgh, Perth, Stirling and Aberdeen as a warning to other would-be traitors.

1460
ON THE IRRESISTIBILITY OF HUMAN FLESH

The 16th-century historian Lindsay of Pitscottie recounts that around this time a brigand and his family were apprehended in Angus. They had, it seems, developed a taste for devouring their fellow humans, and the younger they were, 'the mair tender and delicious'. For these crimes the brigand, together with his wife and children, were all burnt – with the exception of a young girl no more than a year old. This girl was taken to Dundee, where she was fostered until she reached woman-hood, when she was condemned to burn for the crimes she had committed as an infant. As she approached the place of her execution, she was berated for her sins by a great crowd. Growing angry, she riposted that if they had ever tasted the flesh of men or women, they would think it so delicious that they would never again desist from the pleasure. And so, unrepentant, the woman went to her doom.

1475

REBEL DEFEATED BY ATHOLL BROSE

The Earl of Atholl captured the rebel John MacDonald, Earl of Ross and Lord of the Isles, by a cunning ruse. He had his men fill a well in Skye, from which MacDonald frequently quenched his thirst, with honey and whisky. The latter, falling for the trick, soon became so inebriated that he was easily taken prisoner by his enemies. This at least is the traditional explanation of that quintessential Scottish dessert, Atholl Brose, which consists of honey and whisky mixed with oatmeal.

1486

EARL BEARDIE DOOMED TO PLAY CARDS
FOR ETERNITY

Death of Alexander Lyon, 2nd Lord Glamis, who has passed into legend as 'Earl Beardie'. It was said that Earl Beardie was one night playing cards with his cronies when one of them advised him to stop because the Sabbath was fast approaching. Earl Beardie flew into a fury and swore he would go on playing until the Day of Judgement. Prompted by this cue, the Devil made an appearance and offered to join the game. It is said that the two are still playing cards together in a hidden room in Glamis Castle.

The
SIXTEENTH
Century

1500

GLENCONIE MUIR BURNT BY DRAGON

Sir William Sinclair of Roslin reported the appearance of a fearsome beast in 'Glenconie' (a place whose location is not certain). A kinsman of Lord Lovat was out hunting on the hills 'amang very rank heather' when he heard a noise. It was

> like the call of ane ratch [hunting dog] approaching near and near, while [till] at the last he saw it, and shot at it ane dead straik with ane arrow; where it lap and welterit up and down ane spear length of breadth and length. The heather and bent [grass] being mair nor ane foot of height, it being in the deid thraw, brint [burnt] all to the eird [earth], as it had been muirburn. It was mair nor twa eln [more than two metres] of length, as great as the coist [chest?] of ane man, without feet, having ane mickle fin on ilk side, with ane tail and ane terrible head. His great deer-dogs wald not come near it. It had great speed. They callit it ane dragon.

AN EXPERIMENT IN LANGUAGE DEPRIVATION

Around this time James IV conducted an experiment in language deprivation. His theory was that humanity's 'natural' language was Hebrew, and to prove this he had two infant foundlings stranded on the small island of Inchkeith in the Firth of Forth, accompanied only by a mute nursemaid. Some years later the children were brought back to the mainland, but rather than speaking Hebrew they could only utter nonsensical babble.

1507

ABBOT FLIES OFF WALLS OF STIRLING CASTLE

Father John Damian – the notorious quack, charlatan, alchemist and Abbot of Tongland Abbey – attempted to fly from the ramparts of Stirling Castle, apparently in an effort to impress his patron, James IV. Shortly after take-off Damian ended up in a dunghill with a broken thigh bone. He blamed this ignominious outcome on the feathers he had used in his wings (apparently based on a design by Leonardo da Vinci); he had chosen hens' feathers, and realised too late that hens are creatures who 'covet the middens and not the skies'.

1510
BEAST KILLS THREE MEN WITH ITS TAIL

Based on an account given to him by Sir Duncan Campbell, the historian Hector Boece described a 'terrible beast' that had recently been seen in a loch in Argyll. It was, Boece wrote,

> of the bigness of a greyhound, and footed like a gander. Issuing out of the water early in the morning about midsummer [it] did very easily and without any force or straining of himself overthrow huge oaks with his tail, and therewith killed outright three men that hunted him with three strokes of his said tail, the rest of them saving themselves in trees thereabouts, whilst the aforesaid monster returned to the water. Those that are given to the observation of rare and uncouth sights, believe that this beast is never seen but against some great trouble and mischief to come upon the realm of Scotland.

HELL TO OPEN ITS GATES FOR BLUIDY BELL

At Redkirk on the Solway near Gretna there was once a kirkyard, now overwhelmed by sand and sea. In this kirkyard, one gravestone reputedly bore the following reiver's epitaph:

> Here lyeth I—N BELL, who died in ye yhere MDX, and of his age CXXX yheres.

> Here bluidy Bell, baith skin and bane,
> Lies quietly styll aneath this stane.
> He was a stark moss-trooper bent,
> As ever drave a bout o'er bent.
> He brynt ye Lochwood tower and hall,
> And flang ye lady o'er ye wall,

For whilk ye Johnstone, stout and wyte,
Set Blacketh a' in low by nyght,
Whyle cry'd a voice, as if frae hell,
Haste, open ye gates for *bluidy Bell*.

However, the Scots of this supposed epitaph is not of the period claimed, and is likely to be the confection of an 18th- or 19th-century antiquary.

1513
NEVER ON A MONDAY

On their way to join King James's army, the Sinclairs of Caithness crossed the Ord of Caithness, the pass that separates Caithness from Sutherland to the south. It was a Monday, and they all were dressed in green. It was said that barely a single Sinclair survived the subsequent Battle of Flodden, and for centuries no Sinclair would dress in green or dream of crossing the Ord of Caithness on a Monday.

1515
THE CLATTER OF CONSCIENCE

During the minority of James V, various factions strove to control the regency. Anxious to put an end to discord, Gavin Douglas, Bishop of Dunkeld, travelled to Edinburgh to beg Archbishop James Beaton to try to effect a reconciliation. Beaton, more politician than prelate, fully intended to play an active part in the contentions, and to this end wore a suit of armour underneath his clerical robes. But to Douglas he swore on his soul he knew nothing of the matter, and struck his chest emphatically. This caused his breastplate to ring out, prompting Douglas to observe, 'My lord, your conscience is not guid, for I hear it clattering.' Beaton went on to become Lord Chancellor of Scotland.

1523

LACHLAN THE SHAGGY AND THE
STORY OF LADY'S ROCK

(10 November) Death in Edinburgh of Lachlan Cattanach ('Lachlan the Shaggy') Maclean, 11th Chief of Clan Maclean, murdered at the hands of an unknown assailant. The motive was clear, though. Many years before, Maclean had married Katherine Campbell, sister to the Earl of Argyll, in order to reinforce a Maclean–Campbell alliance, but the marriage was not a happy one. She tried to poison him, and he, for his part, stranded her on a small tidal rock in the Sound of Mull, off his seat at Duart Castle, fully expecting that the sea would rid him of his wife for ever. Accordingly, Maclean sent a message to the Earl of Argyll that his sister had met with a tragic accident. But when he next visited the Earl at Inverary Castle, he was dumbfounded to find his wife there before him, alive and well. She had been rescued by fishermen before the tide could claim her.

Although history does not record the name of Maclean's assassin, it is known that he had been contracted by Sir John Campbell of Cawdor – revenge being a dish, as the saying goes, best eaten cold. The rock where Katherine Campbell was left to die can still be seen from the ferry between Oban and Craignure on Mull. It bears a name that remembers the story: Lady's Rock.

1527

'SCOT' A TERM OF ABUSE IN NEWCASTLE

The deeds of incorporation of the Society of Weavers of Newcastle upon Tyne included an injunction to its members 'To take no Scotsman born to apprentice'. Furthermore, 'any brother calling another "Scot" in malice, should forfeit 6s. 8d. without any forgiveness'.

1544
THE BATTLE OF THE SHIRTS

(15 July) Some 800 Macdonalds and Camerons and Frasers fell on each other between Loch Lochy and Loch Oich. The fighting was so fierce and the day so hot that the clansmen shed their plaids and fought only in their shirts. Still suffering from the heat, they agreed to transfer the action to the shallows of the loch to cool down. By the end of the day, only a dozen men remained alive, while the waters of the loch ran red with blood. The encounter became known as *Blar na Léine*, 'field of the shirts'. That, at least, is the story. The truth is more prosaic: *Blar na Léine* is in fact a corruption of *Blar na Leana*, 'field of the marshy meadow'.

1545
LEGLESS LILLIARD, HEROINE OF ANCRUM MOOR

(27 February) Legend has it that at the Battle of Ancrum Moor a young woman known as 'Fair Maiden Lilliard', seeing her lover cut down by the English, seized his sword and set about to avenge his death. Her feats are recorded on a 'grave' at the battle site:

> Fair Maiden Lilliard
> Lies under this stane:
> Little was her stature,
> But muckle was her fame.
>
> Upon the English loons
> She laid monie thumps,
> An' when her legs were cuttit off
> She fought upon her stumps.

The story is almost certainly apocryphal. The battle was fought at Lilliard's Edge, a placename that long predates 1545. And the folklore of northwestern Europe is full of similar tales.

1546
'STICKIT IS YOUR CARDINAL, AND SALTED LIKE A SOW'

(1 March) Cardinal David Beaton, Archbishop of St Andrews, looked on as the popular reformer George Wishart was burnt at the stake. Before he died, Wishart told Beaton he would shortly appear 'in as much shame as he now shows pomp and vanity'. And so it came to pass. On 29 May a party of Protestants seized St Andrews Castle and killed the cardinal, hanging his body over the battlements by an arm and a leg. Government forces besieged the castle, and the defenders preserved Beaton's body by soaking it in brine – hence the popular chant, 'For stickit is your cardinal, and salted like a sow.' The defenders of the castle (who now included John Knox) were forced to surrender in June 1547, and were sent off to work as French galley slaves.

1547
THE ABBOT OF UNREASON DEFIES THE ARCHBISHOP OF ST ANDREWS

For some suspected heresy, John Hamilton, Archbishop of St Andrews, sent letters of excommunication to Lord Borthwick via an 'apparitor', one William Langlands. When Langlands arrived at Borthwick, he presented the letters to the parish priest and commanded him to publish them in church. At this time the inhabitants of Borthwick Castle were enjoying the festivities overseen by the Abbot of Unreason, the Scottish version of the Lord of Misrule. It was the role of the Abbot to subvert all authority, particularly that of the Church, and to mock its rituals. To this end the Abbot descended upon the parish church, seized the unfortunate Langlands and dragged him to the mill pond by the castle, and there forced him to jump in. But the Abbot concluded that the apparitor had not been sufficiently bathed, and so ordered his followers to 'duck him in the most satisfactory and perfect manner' in the mill stream. Langlands was then dragged back to the church, where the Abbot tore up the letters, dunked them in a bowl of wine, and obliged the apparitor to swallow them down. Langlands was then sent on his way, with the warning that if he should return with any more letters during the rule of the Abbot of Unreason, they would 'a' gang the same gait'.

1560
DEADLY TRANSVESTISM IN LEITH

As an English force laid siege to the French garrison of Leith, some of the French soldiers put on women's clothing and made a sortie out of a side gate. Assuming that these dainty dames were ladies of the night, an English sentry strolled over to better make their acquaintance. Imagine his surprise, therefore, when the ladies drew their swords and struck off his head. They then stuck the head on top of a church spire as a warning to others.

1561
APPRENTICES RIOT IN DEFENCE OF
LORD OF INOBEDIENCE

As noted above, in many parts of Scotland, May Day was traditionally celebrated with festivities under the direction of a Lord of Misrule, sometimes in the guise of an 'Abbot of Unreason', sometimes in the guise of Robin Hood. With the Reformation, such goings-on were frowned upon by the upper and middle classes, and a law was enacted to suppress them. However, the workers and tradespeople of the towns were defiant. In April 1561, for example, one George Dune was chosen in Edinburgh as Robin Hood and 'Lord of Inobedience'. The *Diurnal of Occurrents* recounts that on Sunday, 12 May, Dune

> and a great number of other persons came riotously into the city, with an ensign and arms in their hands, in disregard of both the Act of Parliament and an Act of the town-council. Notwithstanding an effort of the magistrates to turn them back, they passed to the Castle Hill, and thence returned at their own pleasure. For this offence a cordiner's [shoemaker's] servant, named James Gillon, was condemned to be hanged on the 21st of July.

Why Gillon should have been picked out for persecution is unclear, but when the day of his doom arrived, a crowd of apprentices and journeymen took up arms, locked the provost and the baillies in a booth, broke down the gallows at the Cross and then proceeded to the Tolbooth prison. Here they battered down the door with hammers, freeing not only Gillon but also the other prisoners in residence. Fighting between the crowd and the forces of authority – involving not only stone throwing but also gunfire – continued for some five hours, until the apprentices and journeymen agreed to disband in return for a promise that they would not face any charges, now or in the future, arising from the day's events.

1562

LOVESICK POET FOUND UNDER QUEEN'S BED

The youthful French poet Pierre de Bocosel de Chastelard was among the French courtiers who accompanied Mary Queen of Scots on her voyage back to Scotland in 1561. According to the unreliable memoirs of Pierre de Bourdeille, Seigneur de Brantôme, the young poet and the Queen exchanged verses, and the Queen encouraged greater intimacy. Whether or not this was indeed the case, the English diplomat Thomas Randolph tells us that Chastelard was found hiding under the Queen's bed at Holyroodhouse, and repeated the outrage on St Valentine's Day 1562 at Rossend Castle in Burntisland. The Queen demanded on the second occasion that her half-brother, the Earl of Moray, kill Chastelard on the spot. However, the poet was taken instead to St Andrews for trial. Chastelard insisted he had been in the Queen's privy, not under her bed. This nice distinction cut no ice with the court, and Chastelard was beheaded at the Market Cross in St Andrews.

EMBALMED CORPSE PUT ON TRIAL FOR TREASON

(28 October) At Corrichie, on the Hill of Fare in Aberdeenshire, the rebel Earl of Huntly met with the Queen's army under the command of the Earl of Moray. Huntly was buoyed up by the prophecies of the witches of Strathbogie, who had told him he would that night lie in the Tolbooth of Aberdeen without a scratch on his body. The witches proved correct. After his defeat, while attempting to surrender, Huntly

suffered a stroke and fell from his horse 'stark dead'. His body was taken to Aberdeen in a couple of fish baskets, and that night laid out in the Tolbooth. The corpse was subsequently embalmed, and then put on trial for treason. It was another three years until the Earl was laid to rest in Elgin Cathedral.

CURES FOR BODIES RUN THROUGH WITH SWORDS

The Council awarded the sum of 20 merks to Robert Henderson, a surgeon, for some remarkable cures that he had wrought, 'viz. on a person whose hands were cut off, a man and a woman run through their bodies with swords by the French, and a woman (said to have been worried [stabbed]) after she was buried, and lyen two days in the grave.'

1563
KNOX SEES HAND OF GOD IN FAMINE

Henry Sinclair, Bishop of Ross and President of the Court of Session, suffering terrible pain from 'the stone', travelled to France in order to seek relief at the hands of the renowned Parisian surgeon Laurentius. The removal of kidney or gall stones was one of the earliest internal operations undertaken by surgeons, and was sometimes successful (Samuel Pepys survived his lithotomy a century later), but in this case the bishop fell into a fever after the operation and died. John Knox noted with some satisfaction that 'God strake him according to his deservings.'

Knox was a great one for noting the hand of God at work. This same year the harvest was poor, and hunger stalked the land. The famine was most severe in the north, where, Knox pointed out, the Catholic Queen Mary had gone on a royal progress the previous autumn. The connection was clear to the great reformer:

> So did God, according to the threatening of his law, punish the idolatry of our wicked Queen, and our ingratitude, that suffered her to defile the land with that abomination [the mass] again . . . The riotous feasting used in court and country wherever that wicked woman repaired, provoked God to

strike the staff of breid, and to give his malediction upon the fruits of the earth.

God's displeasure extended to the whole of Scotland the following January, when Knox recorded:

> God from heaven, and upon the face of the earth, gave decla-ration that he was offended at the iniquity that was committed within this realm; for, upon the twentieth day of January, there fell weet in great abundance, whilk in the falling freezit so vehemently, that the earth was but ane sheet of ice. The fowls both great and small freezit, and micht not flie: mony died, and some were taken and laid beside the fire, that their feathers might resolve. And in that same month, the sea stood still, as was clearly observed, and neither ebbed nor flowed the space of twenty-four hours.

1564
THE DEVIL GETS KNOX A TEENAGE WIFE

(26 March) John Knox, now in his 50s and so regarded as 'ane auld decrepit creature', married for a second time. This time his bride was the 17-year-old Margaret Stewart, a member of the royal house and a distant relative of the Queen. The disparity of ages and of social rank caused tongues to wag. The Catholic propagandist Nicol Burne, for example, speculated

> that sic ane noble house could not have degenerate sae far, except John Knox had interposed the power of his master the Devil, wha, as he transfigures himself sometimes as ane angel of licht, sae he causit John Knox appear ane of the maist noble and lusty men that could be found in the warld.

Knox proved lusty enough, for Margaret bore him three children.

1567

ONE EARL POISONS ANOTHER

Death, by foul means, of the Earl and Countess of Sutherland, the life-long enemy of George Sinclair, 4th Earl of Caithness. Caithness had recruited his cousin, Isobel Sinclair, to poison Sutherland and his wife while they dined at Helmsdale in July 1567. This plot was successful, and Sutherland and the Countess died five days later. Apparently Isobel's son John, unaware of her plan, called for a drink while his mother was preparing the poison, and a servant, equally unaware of what was afoot, brought him the poisoned wine, which he drank. He died two days later. Subsequently Caithness, in order to distract attention from his own guilt, arrested and executed some of the servants of the Earl of Sutherland, accusing them of the crime. However, the death of Isobel's son pointed to her involvement, and she was sent to Edinburgh for trial. There she was found guilty and sentenced to death, but on the day of her execution she was found dead in her cell.

Caithness had not finished with the Sutherlands. He abducted the dead Earl's successor, a 15-year-old boy, and married him to his 32-year-old daughter, Lady Barbara Sinclair. But his plan to kill off the young Earl and marry his second son William to the Earl's elder sister came to naught when Sutherland escaped from Dunrobin Castle. In revenge, Caithness sent his eldest son John, Master of Caithness, to attack the Murrays of Dornoch, firm supporters of Sutherland. Besieged in Dornoch Castle, the Murrays capitulated, and agreed to leave Sutherland within three months, surrendering three hostages as surety. Caithness was furious with the leniency shown by his son; he had expected him to extirpate the entire population of Dornoch while he had the opportunity. The Earl not only beheaded the three hostages, but had a party of armed men seize his son John, who had dared to make a treaty with the Earl's sworn enemies. The Master of Caithness was bound in irons and thrust into a dark dungeon in Castle Girnigoe (aka Castle Sinclair) near Wick, where he was kept for seven long years by his relatives David and Ingram Sinclair. Eventually his keepers decided to end his misery in as miserable a way as they could conceive. To this purpose they deprived him of food for some days, then gave him a large dish of salt beef, 'and then withholding all drink from him, left him to die of raging thirst'.

LAIRD OFFERS HALF HIS LAND IN RETURN FOR ABOLITION OF HELL

Nigel Ramsay, laird of Dalhousie, went to hear a preacher expound on the new reformed faith. Afterwards the Regent Moray, who had listened to the same sermon, asked Ramsay how it had pleased him. 'Passing well,' replied Ramsay. 'Purgatory he hath altogether ta'en away. If the morn he will take away the place of future punishment altogether as well, I will give him half the lands of Dalhousie.'

1568

LYON KING OF ARMS HANGED AS NECROMANCER

Sir William Stewart of Luthrie, Lyon King of Arms, was hanged in St Andrews 'for divers points of witchcraft and necromancy'. He had, the charges against him stated, summoned up a spirit called Obirion, whose picture he had inscribed on a lead tablet alongside the words '*servitus pulcher*', Latin for 'beautiful servant'. He had also practised, the charges stated, various divination techniques, such as that involving a sieve and shears, which convinced him that the Regent Moray would shortly be dead, and that the deposed Mary Queen of Scots would escape from captivity, reassume the throne, and marry Stewart himself, whose children she would bear. Amongst the evidence brought against him was a letter in which he confessed to having consulted a prophet, perhaps Napier of Merchistoun (father of the mathematician). The fact that he was hanged rather than burnt suggests that he was convicted of treason rather than witchcraft. His trial was overseen by the Regent Moray himself, and during the latter's circuit tour, according to the *Diurnal of Occurrents*, 'he causit burn certain witches in Sanctandrois, and in returning he causit burn ane other company of witches in Dundee'. Stewart's prognostications were partially correct: Mary did escape from Loch Leven Castle, and briefly reassumed power before her defeat at Langside and flight into England. However, she never did marry Stewart, or bear his children. Stewart was also right about Moray: in 1570 he was assassinated in Linlithgow.

1570

ABBOT BASTED IN THE BLACK
VAULT OF DUNURE

The most notorious crime of the despotic Gilbert Kennedy, 4th Earl of Carrick, was that involving Master Allan Stewart, notional Abbot of Crossraguel Abbey. Stewart's misfortune was that he had something Kennedy wanted: the revenues of the abbey. So Kennedy lured Stewart to Dunure Castle, where he was held against his will, although 'honourably entertained' – at least for a while. But when Kennedy's blandishments and hospitality failed to achieve the desired result, Stewart was led to the secret chamber known as the Black Vault, which had nothing in it, according to Stewart's own account, but 'a great iron chimney, under it a fire'. Here Kennedy once more presented Stewart with the necessary papers for signature, which would give him the entire benefits of Crossraguel. Stewart again declined, and so Kennedy 'commandit his cooks to prepare the banquet':

> And so first they flayit the sheep, that is, they took off the Abbot's claithes, even to his skin; and next they band him to the chimney, his legs to the one end and his arms to the other; and so they began to beat the fire, sometimes to his buttocks, sometimes to his legs, sometimes to his shoulders and arms. And that the roast should not burn, but that it might roast in sop they spared not flamming with oil. (Lord, look thou to sic cruelty!) And, that the crying of the miserable man sould not be heard, they closed his mouth ... In that torment they held the poor man, while that ofttimes he cried for God's sake to dispatch him; he had as meikle gold in his awn purse as wald buy powder eneugh to shorten his pain.

The Earl in this manner achieved his aim. Stewart complained to the Privy Council, but they were at this time weak, and the force of law did not extend to Carrick. So Kennedy kept the lands, though he gave his victim some money to live upon, 'whilk contentit him all his days'.

MONSTROUS FISH SEEN WEARING
TWO CROWNS

'In this time there was ane monstrous fish seen in Loch Fyne, having great een in the head thereof, and at some times wald stand aboon the water as high as the mast of a ship,' reported the *Diurnal of Occurrents*. The creature apparently bore two crowns on its head, 'whilk was reportit by wise men, that the same was ane sign and taiken of ane sudden alter-ation within this realm'. The allusion was to the recent deposition of Queen Mary, and her replacement on the throne by her infant son James.

PRICKIT WITH THE JUDGMENTS OF GOD,
MINISTER CONFESSES TO MURDERING WIFE

John Kello, minister of Spott in East Lothian, was hanged for murder. Presumably the parish provided but slim pickings, as Kello conceived a plan to kill his own wife, so enabling him to marry more advanta-geously. He pondered how to go about it for 40 days, tried poison unsuccessfully, then settled on strangulation. The deed having been done, he slipped out of the house and went to the church, where he delivered a sermon. On his way back home, he invited some neigh-bours to come and visit his wife, and when he came to the door of his house, he called for her to let them in, 'but nae answer was made':

> Then he passed to another back passage with the neighbours, and that was fund open, and she hinging stranglit at the roof of the house. Then, with admiration, he cryit, as though he had knawn naething of the purpose, and they for pity in like manner cryit out. But, in [the] end, finding himself prickit with the judgments of God, of the grievous punishment wherewith transgressors have been plagued in time bygane, he thought gude to communicate his fact to ane of his brether in office, wha then was schoolmaster at Dunbar.

Plunged into contrition and misery, Kello was persuaded that his only salvation was to come clean. The consequence was inevitable:

> Briefly, by his awn confession, being clearly convict, he was condemnit to be hangit, and his body to be casten in the fire

and brynt to ashes, and so to die without any burial. And thus
he departit this life, with an extreme penitent and contrite
heart, baith for this and all other his offences in general, to the
great gude example and comfort of all beholders.

MAIDEN'S LEAP SAVES HONOUR

Ruthven Castle near Perth, now known as Huntingtower, has two
towers some ten feet apart, although this gap was closed by further
building works in the 17th century. There is a story that a daughter of
Lord Ruthven, 1st Earl of Gowrie, was enamoured with a young
serving man, and one night visited him in the servants' quarters in the
Eastern Tower via the wooden bridge that linked the two. Her mother,
the Countess, was alerted by another servant of this irregular conduct,
and hastened across the bridge to interrupt the illicit tryst. The daughter,
hearing her mother's footsteps on the bridge, rushed to the roof of the
Eastern Tower, and from there made a daring leap across the abyss to
the Western Tower, and so returned to her own bed – where her
mother found her a little later. The next night the young couple eloped
together, and no more was ever heard of them.

1571

JOHN KNOX RAISES THE DEVIL

A rumour spread about that John Knox had been banished from St
Andrews 'because in his yard he had raised some sancts, among whom
came up the Devil with horns'. This had so affrighted his servant
Richard Bannatyne, it was said, that the poor man had 'run mad'. The
previous year another rumour had circulated regarding Knox, to wit
he had been struck by apoplexy and had 'become the most deformed
creature that ever was seen; that his face was turned awry to his neck;
and that he would never preach or speak again'.

1574

DR HANDIE DEPRIVES THE CROWD OF
THEIR PLEASURES

Robert Drummond, known for reasons unknown as 'Dr Handie', had been 'a great seeker and apprehender of papists' in Edinburgh. But his own domestic arrangements fell short of expectations, and his abandonment of his wife to consort with another woman resulted in his exposure in church and his banishment from the city. His services against popery earned him a pardon, but his persistence in his adultery led to him being sentenced to be put in the stocks at the Mercat Cross, and to have his cheek burnt. But before this sentence could be carried out, the furious Drummond shouted out at the gawping crowd, 'What wonder ye? I sall give you more occasion to wonder.' And with that he drew out a knife and struck himself three or four times in the heart, to fatal effect.

1575

THE FOUR-EYED CALF OF ROSLIN

(30 March) At Roslin a calf was born with four eyes, three ears and two mouths. Four centuries later the Roslin Institute was to witness the birth of another prodigy, the world's first cloned mammal, Dolly the Sheep.

1576

BESSIE DUNLOP AND THE GOOD FOLK OF ELFHAME

Bessie Dunlop, a married woman of a certain age from Monkcastle in Ayrshire, came under suspicion for her ability to recover lost or stolen items, and for her cures for difficult diseases. When brought to trial and interrogated as to where she had obtained these powers, she said it was from one Tom Reid, who had died at the Battle of Pinkie 29 years previously. It was, she said, when she was driving her cows to pasture that she had first encountered this respectable, elderly, grey-bearded (if ghostly) gentleman, who bore with him a white wand. She was, she said, in low spirits, crying for her cow that was dead, her husband and child that were lying sick, and she just risen out of child-bed. It was then that Tom Reid accosted her, and asked her what the trouble was. When she told him, he replied that she had irritated God by asking him for something she should not have done. He went on to tell her that her child would die, as would her two sheep, but her husband would recover. Reid, according to Bessie's account, then slipped through a narrower hole in the wall than any earthly man could have gone through. It is not quite clear which of Tom Reid's predictions came to pass, but it appears that at least her husband recovered.

The next time Bessie met Tom Reid, he asked her if she would not trust in him, and she replied that she would trust anybody who did her good. Tom then promised her all kinds of fine stuff, plus horses and cattle, if she would renounce her faith, but this she refused to do. At their next encounter, he introduced her to a group of gentlefolk, eight women and four men, who greeted her and asked her if she would go with them, but she declined. Then they departed, 'and ane hideous ugly sough of wind followit them', and she lay sick till Tom returned. When she asked him who they were, he answered that they were the good people of the Court of Elfhame, the home of the fairies, who had come to ask her to go with them. Tom urged her to follow their bidding, but she would not, as she could not leave her husband and children. At this, Tom 'began to be very crabbit with her', and told her she would 'get little gude of him'.

Despite this threat, Tom continued to give her advice in the preparation of medicines, and Bessie seems to have had some success in treating a variety of cases. She also seems to have had a talent for recovering lost or stolen property, and was consulted on such matters by a variety of folk, including Lady Thirdpart in the barony of Renfrew and Burgess William Kyle of Irvine.

Tom persisted in his attempts to persuade Bessie to join him in Elfhame, and once she met him as she and her husband were riding to Leith to bring home meal. Just as they passed Restalrig Loch, a great company of riders hurtled past them 'and incontinent they rade into the loch, with mony hideous rumble'. Tom told her 'it was the gude wights that were riding in middle-eard'.

The court was clearly impressed by Bessie's story, and sentenced her to die a witch's death in the flames.

1577

THE MONK-LIKE MERMEN OF FORTH

In his *Chronicles* Ralph Holinshed describes how every now and again the Firth of Forth was visited by

> sundry fishes of a monstrous shape, with cowls hanging over their heads like unto monks, and in the rest resembling the body of man. They shew themselves above the water to the navel, howbeit they never appear but against some great pestilence of men or murrain of cattle; wherefore their only sight doth breed great terror to the Scottish nation, who are very great observers of uncouth signs and tokens.

1579

A LAW AGAINST FOOLS, BARDS AND VAGABOND SCHOLARS

Parliament passed an act against the 'undeserving' poor, to wit:

> Strang and idle beggars;
>   Sic as make themselves fules and are bards;
>   The idle people calling themselves Egyptians [i.e. gypsies], or any other that feigns them to have knowledge of charming, prophecy, or other abused sciences, whereby they persuade the people that they can tell their weirds [fates], deaths, and fortunes, and sic other fantastical imaginations;
>   Minstrels, sangsters, and tale-tellers, not avowed in special service by some of the lords of parliament or great burghs;
>   Vagabond scholars of the universities of St Andrews, Glasgow, and Aberdeen.

The 'deserving poor', on the other hand, were to return to their own parishes, where they were to be accommodated in almshouses. Except there were no almshouses.

1581

SINGING OF CAROLS PUNISHABLE BY DEATH

Parliament passed a law banning many traditional religious practices and observations, such as Christmas. In particular the 'singing of carolis within and about kirkis at certain seasonis of the yeir' was forbidden. Anyone enjoying themselves in such a manner would be fined, and if they repeated the offence they were 'to suffer the pain of deid as idolatoris'.

1584

SATAN URGES BOY TO START FIRE

A contemporary chronicler relates how a boy called Robert Henderson

> desperately put some powder and a candle in his father's heather-stack, standing in a close opposite to the Tron of Edinburgh, and burnt the same, with his father's house, which lay next adjacent, to the imminent hazard of burning the whole town. For which, being apprehended most marvel-lously, after his escaping out of the town, he was on the next day burnt quick at the Cross, as an example.

The chronicler says the boy was no doubt prompted 'by the instigation of Satan'.

1585

BANISHMENT TO GLASGOW:
A FATE WORSE THAN DEATH?

A tailor called David Duly was convicted of failing to report the death of his wife from the plague to the city authorities of Edinburgh. He was sentenced to be hanged outside his own house, but the rope broke. Taking this as a sign of heaven's purpose in the matter, the court commuted Duly's sentence, and rather than being hanged he was banished to Glasgow.

QUEEN'S LIPS MOVE AFTER HEAD CUT OFF

(8 February) Execution of Mary Queen of Scots at Fotheringhay Castle. A certain 'Ro. Wy.' (probably Robert Wingfield) left an eye-witness account, in which he reported that 'Her lips stirred up and down for a quarter of an hour after her head was cut off.' He also relates how Mary's little dog had crept under her clothes and 'could not be got forth but by force, yet afterwards would not depart from the dead corpse but came and lay between her head and her shoulders'.

1590

DEAD MAN'S MOUTH STUFFED WITH
BREAD AND CHEESE

John Drummond of Drummond-Ernoch, keeper of the royal forest in Glenartney, had the responsibility of dealing with the poaching activities of the neighbouring MacGregors, several of whose ears he had cut off. In retaliation, one day a band of MacGregors ambushed Drummond as he was gathering venison for the return of King James VI from Denmark with his new bride. They struck off his head, wrapped it in a plaid, and carried it off as a trophy. Passing the house of Drummond's sister at Ardvorlich, they dropped in and were offered – as was the custom of the Highlands – bread and cheese by the lady of the house. As she went back to the kitchen to find more food to offer her guests, they placed their gruesome cargo on the table, unwrapped it, and placed a piece of bread and cheese in its mouth. 'Go on and eat,' one MacGregor mocked, 'as you have often eaten in this house before.' At that moment Drummond's sister returned, saw the hideous relic of her brother, and fled from the house. She was only 'recovered to her home and sanity with great difficulty'. The assassins meanwhile had taken the head back to their chief in Balquhidder. The chief then summoned all the menfolk of the clan to the church, where each man touched the head in turn, swearing that the slaughter had been carried out with their sanction and approval, and vowing to defend the actual murderers with all the strength at their disposal. When all this was reported to the Privy Council, letters of fire and sword were issued against the wrongdoers, who were soon afterwards captured and hanged.

1592
WARLOCK RAISES DEVIL FOR THE JUSTICE CLERK

Richard Graham, a noted warlock, was strangled and burnt at the Cross of Edinburgh. It had been widely reported that Sir Lewis Bellenden, the Justice Clerk, had requested Graham to raise the Devil. This Graham did, in Bellenden's own yard in the Canongate, Edinburgh. According to *The Staggering State of Scottish Statesmen* written by Sir John Scot of Scotstarvit in the 1650s, Bellenden 'was thereby so terrified, that he took sickness and there died'.

1593
END OF THE WORLD PREDICTED

Publication of *A Plaine Discovery of the Whole Revelation of St John* by John Napier, better remembered today for his invention of logarithms. Napier himself regarded his most important work to be his study of the Book of Revelation, which, together with the Sibylline Books of ancient Rome, he used to predict the date of the end of the world. Satan's bondage, he calculated, had begun in AD 300, and ended in 1300, and thereafter the Devil had been busy stirring up trouble between the armies of Gog (the Pope) and Magog ('the Turkes and Mahometanes'). The seventh trumpet, he believed, had sounded in 1541, signalling the 'Third woe'. From all this he calculated that the end of the world would take place sometime between 1688 and 1700.

1595
THE RISE AND FALL OF THE ORIGINAL LADY MACBETH

Death of Elizabeth Stewart, Countess of Arran, the possible model for Shakespeare's Lady Macbeth. The daughter of the Earl of Atholl, she had six children by her first husband, Hugh Fraser, Lord Lovat, who died in 1577. She then married Robert Stewart, Earl of Lennox, then in his fifties, but in 1581 she had the marriage annulled on account of his reputed impotence. Less than two months later she married her lover, Captain James Stewart, who had just been made Earl of Arran, and by whom she was then pregnant.

During the minority of James VI, the Earl of Arran was one of the most powerful men in the country. This made Elizabeth the first lady at court, which attracted considerable envy and not a little hatred, not least because she had a manner that was at once coarse and haughty. Many rumours were circulated by her enemies: that she had pawned one of the crown jewels; that she and her husband were responsible for an outbreak of plague in Edinburgh and the failure of crops round-about; that she would interfere in legal cases to her own benefit. One contemporary writer records that she offered pardons to condemned men in return for a suitable consideration; if they failed to comply, she would have them hanged. 'What had they been doing all their days,' she would say, 'that had not so much as five punds to buy them from the gallows?' The same writer calls her 'the maistresse of all vice and villany', and says she 'infectit the air in his Hieness' audience'. One of her husband's principal enemies, the Earl of Gowrie, described her as 'a vile and impudent woman, over famous for her monstrous doings, not without suspicion of the devilish magical art'. Indeed, one of the most persistent stories about the Countess was that she consorted with witches, and boasted that they had told her she would be the greatest woman in Scotland. The Lovat family chronicler recorded her death in 1595, somewhat gleefully observing that the witches' prophecy had been fulfilled – for the Countess died with her body horribly swollen by the dropsy.

Arran himself was murdered that same year by Sir James Douglas of Parkhead, nephew of Regent Morton, in whose fall Arran had played a prominent part. Hearing that the Earl was travelling through his part of Lanarkshire, Parkhead set off in pursuit, caught up with his quarry, felled him from his horse and killed him. He then had one of his servants mount Arran's head upon a spear, fulfilling another prophecy: that he would one day have the highest head in Scotland.

SCHOOLBOYS SHOOT BAILLIE
DURING ARMED SIEGE

In September 1595 Hercules Rollock, the rector of the Royal High School in Edinburgh, upset the students under his charge. The council had given Rollock the task of instructing his pupils in 'piety, good manners, doctrine and letters', but the youths had been slack in their studies, and Rollock declined their request to grant the traditional autumn holiday. In retaliation, a group of pupils staged a sit-in, arming themselves with food, drink, hagbuts, pistols and swords. After they refused entry to Rollock, the authorities were called in, and Baillie John Macmorran led a party of men to force an entrance. As Macmorran approached, William Sinclair, one of the revolting youths, vowed to God that he would shoot a pair of bullets through his head, and with that blew out a window with one shot, and the brains of Macmorran with another. Sinclair and seven of his fellows were arrested and thrown into jail, but complained to King James VI that as they were the scions of noble and landowning families, the city magistrates had no jurisdiction over them. They requested that they instead be tried by their peers. This request appears to have been granted, as the boys were later released. Rector Rollock was not so lucky, being dismissed from his post. After his departure, in his own words, the High School sank once more 'into the barbarism from which he recovered it'. As for Macmorran's killer, in due course he became Sir William Sinclair of Mey.

1596

EDINBURGH ASTONISHED BY HORSE OF WONDERFUL CAPABILITIES

In April of this year, an Englishman called William Bankes and his horse Marocco put on a performance in Edinburgh. The performance was described by Patrick Henderson, one of the audience, in his *History of Scotland*:

> ... he made him to do many rare and uncouth tricks, such as never horse was observed to do the like before in this land. This man would borrow from twenty or thirty of the specta-tors a piece of gold or silver, put all in a purse, and shuffle them together; thereafter he would bid the horse give every gentleman his own piece of money again. He would cause him tell by so many pats with his foot how many shillings the piece of money was worth. He would cause him lie down as dead. He would say to him: 'I will sell you to a carter:' then

he would seem to die. Then he would say: 'Marroco, a gentleman hath borrowed you, and you must ride with a lady of court.' Then would he most daintily hackney, amble, and ride a pace, and trot, and play the jade at his command when his master pleased. He would make him take a great draught of water as oft as he liked to command him. By a sign given him, he would beck for the King of Scots and for Queen Elizabeth, and when ye spoke of the King of Spain, would both bite and strike at you – and many other wonderful things. I was a spectator myself in those days. But the report went afterwards that he devoured his master, because he was thought to be a spirit and nought else.

Marocco had not devoured his master, and the two later toured France, where in Paris the horse's uncanny abilities attracted accusation of sorcery against his master, obliging Bankes to reveal how the tricks were achieved. Moving on to Orléans, Bankes was found guilty of witch craft and sentenced to burn at the stake, but obtained an acquittal when he persuaded Marocco to kneel before a cross held up by a priest, to show that neither horse nor master were of the Devil's party.

WOMEN OBLIGED TO PAY FOR THEIR OWN EXECUTION

In Aberdeen two women, Janet Wishart and Isabel Crocker, prior to being burnt for witchcraft, were presented with a bill for £11 10s, to cover the expenses of their execution. The bill itemised such things as 20 loads of peat, four tar barrels, four fathoms of rope and a stake (dressed), plus transportation costs and the justice's fee for overseeing the proceedings.

1597

DEVIL LEADS CATS AND HARES IN DANCE ROUND THE CROSSES

(23 February) Thomas Lees, the son of the convicted witch Janet Wishart (see above), was brought to trial in Aberdeen. It was alleged that he had been one of a great party of witches and sorcerers who had assembled at midnight on the previous Halloween at the Fish and Market Crosses, 'under the guiding and conduct of the Devil . . . playing before you on his kind of instruments'. Some of the company were transformed into cats, others into hares, others into different guises, in which for a long space of time they danced around the Crosses. One of the participants, Catherine Mitchell, told the court how Lees had beat her to make her dance faster, while another woman testified that Lees had promised to marry her, and told her how he would raise a spirit to supply them with all that would be needed for their comfort. Like his mother, Lees was condemned to burn.

WOMEN SWOON AS ECLIPSE TAKEN FOR DAY OF JUDGEMENT

(25 February) A natural phenomenon caused widespread alarm, as recorded by David Calderwood in his *Historie of the Kirk of Scotland* (1646):

> Betwixt nine and ten forenoon, began a fearful eclipse which continued about two hours. The whole face of the sun seemed to be covered and darkened about half a quarter of an hour, in such measure that none could see to read a book. The stars appeared in the firmament. Sea, land and air were still, and stricken dead as it were. The ravens and fowls flocking together, mourned exceedingly in their kind. Great multitudes of paddocks [frogs] ran together, making an uncouth and hideous noise; men and women were astonished, as if the day of judgement had been coming. Some women swooned. The streets of Edinburgh were full of cries. Some men ran off the streets to the kirk to pray.

THOUSANDS ATTEND BLACK SABBATH IN ATHOLL

Execution of Margaret Aiken, known as 'the Great Witch of Balwery'. Under torture, she told her inquisitors how she had attended a black sabbath on a hill in Atholl along with 'twenty-three hundred' other persons, including the Devil. As a consequence, 'There was many of them tried by swimming in the water, by binding of their two thumbs and their great toes together, for, being thus casten in the water, they floated ay aboon.' Aiken said that those who were witches had a secret mark in their eyes, which she could detect, and thus she found her services much in demand by the gullible. She was taken around the country identifying witches, and as a consequence several innocent old women were put to death. Aiken was only exposed when certain persons whom she one day declared to possess the demonic mark appeared before her again the following day, in different clothes, and this time she proclaimed them innocent.

HUSBANDS BLAME WITCH FOR THEIR OWN ADULTERY

In Aberdeen, two men accused a certain Helen Fraser of having used the dark arts to transfer their affections from their own wives to other women. One of the men, Andrew Tullideff, testified that Helen 'sae michtily bewitchit' him that he fell for a certain Margaret Neilson, and that 'he could never be reconceillit with his wife, or remove his affection frae the said harlot'. Another man, Robert Merchant, said that he had been married for two years to Christian White, but then he went to sow corn for a widow called Isobel Bruce at Muirhill of Foveran (where Helen Fraser was at that time living) and he 'fand his affection violently and extraordinarily drawn away from the said Christian to the said Isobel'. The court agreed with this explanation of the unfaithfulness of the two husbands, and Helen Fraser was dispatched to the flames.

MEN DUEL TO THE DEATH OVER NUMBER OF SACRAMENTS

A disagreement broke out between James Hepburn of Moreham and an Edinburgh skinner called Birnie over the number of sacraments. Hepburn insisted there were seven, while Birnie held there were but two. A duel ensued, fought on 11 March at St Leonard's Crags. Both men were killed, and were buried the following morning.

The
SEVENTEENTH
Century

1600

PUNISHMENT FOR SUICIDES

(20 February) A contemporary chronicler recorded the following sad tale:

> Thomas Dobbie drowned himself in the Quarry Holes, besyde the Abbey [at Holyrood]; and upon the morn he was harilt [hauled] through the town backward, and thereafter hangit on the gallows.

REIVER INSULTED BY EGG YOLKS ON HIS SWORD

Hearing that Sir John Carmichael, Warden of the West Marches, was about to hold a Warden's Court in Lochmaben with the intention of doling out severe punishments for the recent forays and thefts committed by the Armstrongs, Alexander Armstrong (brother of Kinmont Willie, hero of the eponymous ballad) went to visit Carmichael, in the hope of coming to an amicable settlement. However, Carmichael soon made it clear that there was going to be no leniency. To add insult to injury, some of Carmichael's retainers slipped Armstrong's sword out of its scabbard and covered the blade with egg yolks, so that when sheathed it would not draw. Furious, Armstrong returned home and told his son Thomas what had transpired. Next day, 16 June 1600, Thomas and his brothers accosted Carmichael, and shot him with a hagbut. Thomas did not long evade justice. He was tried and convicted in Edinburgh on 14 November, and before he was hanged his right hand was cut off. His body was then hung in chains on the Borough Muir, the first recorded instance of a criminal suffering such a fate in Scotland.

WAR OF THE ONE-EYED WOMAN SPREADS ACROSS HEBRIDES

Donald Gorm Mor, chief of the MacDonalds of Sleat on Skye, returned his prospective wife Margaret MacLeod, to her brother, Rory Mor, chief of the MacLeods of Dunvegan. This was in accordance with the custom of the time, described by Martin Martin in his *Description of the Western Isles of Scotland* (1703):

It was an ancient custom in the islands that a man should take a maid to his wife, and keep her the space of a year without marrying her; and if she pleased him all the while, he married her at the end of the year, and legitimated these children; but if he did not love her, he returned her to her parents, and her portion also . . .

Margaret had, indeed, during her stay with Donald, not only failed to conceive a child, she had lost the sight in one of her eyes. Donald, considering her to be damaged goods, mounted her backwards on a one-eyed horse, and had her led back to Dunvegan by a one-eyed groom, accompanied by a one-eyed mongrel dog.

Margaret's family were outraged by the insult, and so began the 'War of the One-Eyed Woman', which lasted for two years, caused much suffering, and spread as far as Trotternish, Harris and South Uist. It came to an end with a decisive MacDonald victory at the Battle of Coire Na Creiche on the northern flanks of the Black Cuillin. The Privy Council ordered the two chiefs to make peace, and, apart from a minor incident in 1603, that was the end of the bloodshed between the MacDonalds and MacLeods on Skye.

1603

A PROPHECY FULFILLED

At Drumelzier, near the supposed grave of Merlin, the River Tweed overflowed into the nearby River Powsail. Many centuries previously Thomas the Rhymer had prophesied that 'When Tweed and Powsail meet at Merlin's grave, England and Scotland shall one monarch have.' And so it turned out. In this very year James VI of Scotland succeeded, on the death of Elizabeth I, to the throne of England.

KING OFFERS TO SHOW SUBJECTS HIS ARSE

After being crowned king of England, James was told that his new subjects wished to see his face. 'God's wounds!' he declared, 'I will pull down my breeches and they shall also see my arse!'

1609

COUNTESS GIVES HUSBAND CANCER

(8 April) Death of Mark Ker, 1st Earl of Lothian. It was said that his wife, Margaret Maxwell, had a hand in his demise, as described by Sir Robert Douglas in his *Peerage of Scotland* (1764):

> That lady thereafter being vexed with a cancer in her breast, implored the help of a notable warlock called Playfair, who condescended to heal her, but with condition that the sore should fall on them she loved best; whereunto she agreeing did convalesce, but the Earl, her husband, found the cancer in his throat, of which he died shortly after.

1611

POLE BEHEADED FOR INSULTING SCOTTISH NATION

John Stercovius, a German resident in Poland, met an unfortunate and unforeseeable end. Some time previously he had visited Scotland wearing his native dress, but was so laughed at, mocked and reviled that he retreated back to Poland. Here he published a *Legend of Reproaches*, in which he vilified the entire Scottish nation. This libel being brought to the attention of James VI, the king mounted an action against Stercovius, via Patrick Gordon, a Scottish agent resident in Danzig. So much pressure was put upon the Polish government that Stercovius was arrested, tried, convicted and beheaded 'by the sword' in Rastenburg.

1612

COW GIVES BIRTH TO PUPPIES

In his *Historie of the Kirk of Scotland* (1646), David Calderwood records the following curious events taking place in this year:

> In the month of March and April fell furth prodigious works and rare accidents. A cow brought forth fourteen great dog

whelps instead of calves . . . One of the Earl of Argyle's servants being sick, vomited two toads and a serpent, and so convalesced: but vomited after a number of little toads.

1616

GYPSIES BANISHED ON PAIN OF DEATH

Four gypsies – John Faa together with his son James and two others, namely Moses Baillie and Helen Brown – were put on trial in Edinburgh 'as Egyptians lingering in the country, contrary to a statute which had banished their tribe forth of the realm on pain of death'. As the accused failed to provide assurances that they would leave the country, they were sentenced to be hanged on the Burgh Muir on the edge of Edinburgh. A similar fate met six more Faas and two other gypsies in 1624, while in 1636 a band of gypsies were rounded up and put into jail in Haddington. The Privy Council, realising that 'the keeping of them longer there is troublesome and burdenable to the town', decreed that the sheriff should pronounce a sentence of death against all the men and any of the women without children, the men to be hanged and the women drowned. Those women with children, the Council mercifully decreed, were to be 'scourged through the burgh'.

1618

DEVIL DISGUISES HIMSELF AS LADY'S LAPDOG

Margaret Barclay, the young and spirited wife of Archibald Deane, a burgess of Irvine, had been accused of some act of theft by her brother-in-law, John Deane, and his wife, Janet Lyal. As a result, Margaret had conceived a loathing for the couple, which she did not care to disguise, even after the local kirk session urged a reconciliation. Shortly thereafter, the *Gift of God*, a ship belonging to John Deane, was lost off Padstow in Cornwall, taking Deane, together with the provost of Irvine and all but two of the crew, to the bottom of the sea. It was remembered by some that as the ship had embarked, Margaret Barclay had muttered prayers that neither sea nor salt water should bear the ship, and that crabs might eat the flesh of all on board at the bottom of the ocean. Suspicions were aroused, especially when one John Stewart, a wandering *spaeman* (soothsayer) who claimed to have contacts in Elfland, spoke of the loss of the ship before it was generally known in Irvine. When Stewart was confronted with accusations of sorcery, he confessed that he had been present on the shore when the Devil, in the guise of a lady's lapdog, had taught Margaret Barclay the dark arts by which she might be revenged upon her slanderers. A model of the ship was made in clay, and, at night, cast into the sea, which promptly began to rage and roar and turn blood red. Another woman, Isobel Insh or Taylor, was implicated by Stewart in assisting Margaret, and Isobel, together with her eight-year-old daughter, who was Margaret's servant girl, was terrorised into supporting Stewart's accusations, the servant girl adding that the lapdog emitted flashes from its jaws and nostrils, enabling the witches to see what they were doing as they went about their work. Things went from bad to worse. Isobel tried to escape from her imprisonment in the church belfry, but, bound as she was in heavy chains, fell from the church roof, and died of her injuries a few days later. Stewart hanged himself while in custody. Margaret Barclay was subjected to what was regarded as 'safe and gentle' torture, great iron weights being laid upon her shins, causing great pain but failing to break the skin. She was thus induced to confess, urged on by the pious persuadings of several local ministers. As she made this confession after the weights had been removed, the jury considered that it was not forced upon her, even though she had subsequently withdrawn her confession. She was duly found guilty. As a benevolent gesture, she was strangled before she was burnt, 'having died with many expressions of religion and penitence'.

1621

REDISTRIBUTION OF WEALTH

A law came into force prohibiting the playing of cards or dice in a house unless the master of the house was himself playing. Furthermore, should anyone win more than 100 merks betting on the horses, or on any other wagers within a 24-hour period, the excess should be distributed among the local poor.

1622

THERE WAS A FIERY DRAGON, BOTH GREAT AND LONG

In his *Historie of the Kirk of Scotland* (1646), David Calderwood records that in this year:

> Upon Monday the 3rd of June, there was a fiery dragon, both great and long, appeared to come from the south to the north, spouting fire from her, half an hour after the going to of the sun.

1623

THE PERILS OF PLACING A HEN UNDER A WOMAN'S ARMPIT

Thomas Grieve was brought before a court in Edinburgh, accused of having cured many people 'of heavy sickness and grievous diseases, by various magical arts'. The court heard how he rid one woman in Leslie, Fife, of her sickness by transferring it to a cow, which then went mad and died. Another woman, the wife of one James Mudie, he treated for fever, affecting a cure

> by causing ane great fire to be put on, and ane hole to be made in the north side of the house, and ane quick hen to be put furth thereat, at three several times, and ta'en in at the house-door withershins; thereafter taking the hen, and putting it under the sick woman's oxter or arm, and therefra carrying it to the fire, where it was halden doun and burnt quick therein.

On the advice of various parish ministers, the court sentenced Grieve to be strangled, then burnt at the stake.

1629

MAN FINED FOR SPEWING

The baron court of the Campbells of Glenorchy fined a man for being sick on someone's floor.

1630

A SHOCKING INSTANCE OF INCEST

Alexander Blair, a tailor from Currie, was beheaded for having married the daughter of the half-brother of his first wife.

1633

GENTLEMEN FIRE ON SLEEPING HIGHLANDERS

Whilst deer-stalking in the wild upper reaches of Strath Avon in Moray, Alexander Gordon of Dunkintie and his son 'suddenly lighted upon a party of natives, believed to be of the Clan Chattan, who were sleeping upon the hillside. Suspecting these men to be rogues, the two gentlemen shot at them . . .' One of the 'natives' was wounded, at which his fellows set upon Gordon and his son, killing both. During the skirmish two more 'natives' were killed, and Dunkintie's servants fled to raise the alarm. Dunkintie's second son, together with a party of retainers, soon arrived at the scene. He had the bodies of his father and brother taken to Elgin for burial, the procession being headed by a servant bearing the severed head of one of the Highlanders on an iron spike.

WITCH-PRICKER PROMISES NEVER TO PRICK AGAIN

John Kincaid, a notorious witchfinder, was tried before the Privy Council for fraud and deceit in his 'work of pricking witches for the Devil's mark'. His method involved searching for unusual blemishes on the skin of a suspect. Once located, he would insert a pin at the place, and if the subject did not feel anything, and there was no blood when the pin was withdrawn, the suspect was found to be guilty of witchcraft. By his own admission, Kincaid was responsible for the deaths of 220 people in Scotland and England. He was imprisoned for pricking without a magistrate's warrant, but was released after nine weeks owing to his great age, and his promise that he would never prick again.

1634

DOGS AS INSTRUMENTS OF JUSTICE – PART I

In Orkney, a youth of 18 years of age called William Garioch was bequeathed some land and some cattle by his late father. At the time the lad was living with his uncle, who coveted his nephew's inheritance, and who kept him on such strict rations that the latter stole some two dozen pounds of barley to keep himself from hunger. The uncle reported the theft to the sheriff, and the youth was seized, put on trial, and sentenced to death. As he mounted the ladder to be hanged, young Garioch prayed loudly that God should visit justice upon his wicked uncle. Some time after the execution, his uncle was walking through the churchyard of Kirkwall, and, as he stood upon his nephew's grave, 'the bishop's dog ran at him all of a sudden, and tore out his throat'.

DOGS AS INSTRUMENTS OF JUSTICE – PART II

(14 December) Death in Stirling of John Erskine, 19th and 2nd Earl of Mar, Lord Treasurer of Scotland. Sir John Scot of Scotstarvit describes the circumstances of his death thus:

> His chief delight was in hunting; and he procured by Acts of Parliament, that none should hunt within divers miles of the king's house; yet often that which is most pleasant to a man is his overthrow; for, walking in his own hall, a dog cast him off his feet, and lamed his leg, of which he died; and at his burial, a hare having run through the company, his special chamberlain, Alexander Stirling, fell off his horse and broke his neck.

GREAT BLAZING STAR BODES ILL FOR SCOTLAND

The contemporary historian John Spalding recorded that 'There was seen in Scotland a great blazing star, representing the shape of a crab or cancer, having long spraings spreading from it.' Various dire circumstances followed. The winter was so cold that snow lay on the lowlands from 9 December 1634 to 9 March the following year. The River Tay was frozen over for 30 consecutive days, while the streets of Perth were buried under some seven feet of snow. With the waters frozen, millers

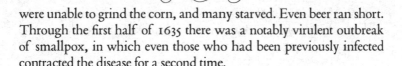

were unable to grind the corn, and many starved. Even beer ran short. Through the first half of 1635 there was a notably virulent outbreak of smallpox, in which even those who had been previously infected contracted the disease for a second time.

1635
MER~PIG SNORTS AND BULLERS IN RIVER DON

In June, just as the smallpox epidemic grew less virulent, another sinister portent shook the northeast, as John Spalding recorded:

> There was seen in the water of Don a monster~like beast, having the head like to ane great mastiff dog or swine, and hands, arms and paps like to a man. The paps seemed to be white. It had hair on the head, and the hinder parts, seen sometimes above the water, seemed clubbish, short~legged, and short~footed, with ane tail. This monster was seen swimming bodily above the water, about ten hours in the morning, and continued all day visible, swimming above and below the bridge without any fear. The town's~people of both Aberdeens came out in great multitudes to see this monster. Some threw stones; some shot guns and pistols; and the salmon~fishers rowed cobbles with nets to catch it, but all in vain. It never shrinked nor feared, but would duck under the water, snorting and bullering, terrible to the hearers and beholders. It remained two days, and was seen no more.

1636
THE AMAZING ADVENTURES OF
PATRICK ROY MACGREGOR

The cattle thief Patrick Roy MacGregor, known as Gilderoy (Gaelic *Gille Ruadh*, 'the red~haired lad'), was hanged in Edinburgh on account of his numerous depredations. His career was subsequently romanticised by the balladeers, and over the following centuries the most improbable tales were being told about him: that he picked the purse of Cardinal Richelieu in sight of the French king; that he stole the valuable plate of the Duke of Medinaceli in Madrid; that he ambushed and robbed Oliver Cromwell himself, then tied him onto a donkey and sent him packing.

1637

PENALTIES IMPOSED FOR TRAVELLING TO IRELAND

A law was introduced stating that any person travelling to Ireland without a licence should be apprehended as a thief.

WOMEN HURL STOOLS AND BIBLES AT
DEAN OF EDINBURGH

(23 July) The imposition of the Prayer Book upon the Church of Scotland by that distant king, Charles I, sparked a riot in the heart of his northern capital. Here is the account given by James Gordon in his *History of Scots Affairs, from 1637 to 1641* of what happened when an attempt was made to use the book for the first time in St Giles, Edinburgh:

> How soon as Dr George Hanna, Dean of Edinburgh, who was to officiate that day, had opened the service-book, a number of the meaner sort of people, most of them waiting-maids and women, who use in that town to keep places for the better sort, with clapping of their hands, cursings and outcries, raised such an uncouth noise and hubbub in the church, that not any one could either hear or be heard. The gentlewomen did fall a tearing and crying that the mass was entered amongst them, and Baal in the church. There was a gentleman standing behind a pew and answering 'Amen' to what the Dean was reading; a she-zealot, hearing him, starts up in choler: 'Traitor,' says she, 'does thou say mass at my ear!' and with that struck him on the face with her Bible in great fury.
>
> The Bishop of Edinburgh, Mr David Lindsay, stepped into the pulpit, above the Dean, intending to appease the tumult, minding them of the place where they were, and entreating them to desist from profaning it. But he met with as little reverence (albeit with more violence) as the Dean had

found; for they were more enraged, and began to throw at him stools, and their very Bibles . . . Nor were their tongues idler than their hands. Upon this, John Spottiswoode, Archbishop of St Andrews, then Lord Chancellor, and some others, offering to assist the Bishop in quelling the multitude, were made partners of the suffering of all these curses and impre⁄cations which they began to pray to the bishops and their abettors. The Archbishop, finding himself unable to prevail with the people, was forced to call down from their gallery the provost and bailies and others of the town council of Edinburgh, who at length, with much tumult and confusion, thrust the unruly rabble out of the church, and made fast the church doors.

The multitude being removed, the Dean falls again to read, in presence of the better sort who stayed behind; but all this while, those who had been turned out of doors, kept such a quarter with clamours without, and rapping at the church doors, and pelting the windows with stones, as that the Dean might once more be interrupted. This put the bailies once more to the pains to come down from their seat, and interpose with the clamorous multitude to make them quiet. In the midst of these clamours, the service was brought to an end; but the people's fury was not a whit settled . . .

Tradition has identified the hurler of the first stool as one Jenny Geddes, although Robert Wodrow (1679–1734), in his unpublished *Analecta*, tells us that others believed it was a certain Mrs Mean, wife of a merchant, and that 'many of the lasses that carried on the fray were prentices in disguise, for they threw stools to a great length'.

1638
GHOSTLY DRUMMING HEARD IN ABERDEENSHIRE

Throughout the winter of 1637–8, numerous witnesses reported that the sound of drumming could be heard on many a night in the vicinity of Barmekin Hill and Loch Skene near Echt in Aberdeenshire. Not only drumming was heard; also the sounds of guards parading to and fro. And those with knowledge of these things swore that they could distinguish the different marches of Scotland, Ireland, England, France, Denmark and Holland. What is more, 'Some gentlemen of known integrity and truth affirmed that, near these places, they heard as perfect shot of cannon go off as ever they heard at the Battle of Nordlingen, where themselves some years before had been present.' All this, in retrospect, was held to foretell the civil wars that were to come.

1639
DOGS SLAIN FOR DISRESPECT

In March an army of 11,000 men under Montrose and Leslie entered Aberdeen to impose the Covenant on its reluctant citizens, who were more inclined to follow the Episcopal principles of the king. The Covenanters wore around their necks their badge of the blue ribbon, and in mockery some of the women of the city put blue ribbons around the necks of their lap dogs – 'whereat the soldiers took offence, and killed all their dogs for this very cause'. The citizens took the hint and swore 'by their uplifted hands to God that they did subscribe and swear this Covenant willingly, freely, and from their hearts, and not from any fear or dread that could happen.'

1640
PILLAR OF FIRE FORETELLS VAST
MUNITIONS EXPLOSION

On 27 August watchers in Fife looking across the Firth of Forth saw, about eight o'clock in the evening, a great pillar of fire rising into the sky from somewhere to the northeast of Dunbar. The pillar gave off a light as bright as a full moon, and rose up to the roof of heaven. Then it slowly faded, and by eleven o'clock had entirely vanished. This strange phenomenon was taken in retrospect as a portent of the events of the following Sunday, when the vast munitions store in the vault of Dunglass Castle in Berwickshire exploded, killing the Earl of Haddington and a dozen other Covenanting commanders, together with more than 50 servants of both sexes. Thirty others were seriously injured. It was thought that the explosion was ignited – either by accident or by design – by an English page, one Edward Paris, whom the Earl had entrusted with a key to the vault. All that was found of this boy was 'ane arm, holding ane iron spoon in his hand'. As for the Earl, King Charles remarked that 'albeit Lord Haddington had been very ungrateful to him, yet he was sorry that he had not at his dying some time to repent'.

1642
MAN WITH TWO HEADS TOURS SCOTLAND

An Italian called Lazare Colloredon Genois toured through Scotland, accompanied by two servants. When he was settled into a lodging, one of the servants would blow a trumpet to summon the local populace, while the other collected money from the curious. When sufficient money had been collected, the Italian would part the voluminous cloak he habitually wore, revealing a twin brother growing out of his chest. This brother, who had been separately baptised under the name Jean-Baptiste, was barely sentient. His head drooped backwards and his eyes remained closed. He had two arms, two hands with three fingers on each, and one leg with six toes, the other leg being concealed within the flesh. Lazare himself appeared perfectly healthy, and was possessed of good manners and a vivacity only occasionally diminished when he dwelt upon his fate should his brother predecease him.

1643
LORDS DRINK A HEALTH TO THE DEVIL

(January) In his *Memorials*, the field preacher Robert Law (d. *c*.1686) recounts how one day a group of five gentlemen, including the Earl of Kelly, Lord Kerr and David Sandilands, brother to Lord Abercrombie, embarked on a marathon drinking session. Toast followed toast until they could not think whom next to toast, so, in Law's words, 'one of them gives the Devil's health, and the rest pledges him'. Law goes on to spell out the consequences:

> Sandilands that night, going downstairs, fell and broke his neck; Kelly and Kerr within a few days sickened of a fever

and died; the fourth also died shortly; and the fifth, being under some remorse, lived some time.

SERVANTS SUBJECTED TO TONSORIAL HUMILIATION

Death of George Sinclair, 5th Earl of Caithness, who turned out to be as unruly and vengeful as his grandfather, the 4th Earl (*see* 1567). Among his many feuds was one with the Earl of Orkney, whom he set out to slight in the following manner. During a terrible storm, a ship bearing some of the Earl of Orkney's servants sought refuge on the coast of Caithness. But rather than offering shelter and hospitality, the Earl had the men taken into custody. They were then forced to drink large quantities of spirits, while having one side of their heads and one side of their beards shaven off. They were then bundled back onto their ship, and obliged to set to sea once more, even though the storm still raged with undiminished fury.

1644

COVENANTERS CRY JESUS AND NO QUARTER!

At the Battle of Tippermuir near Perth, the Covenanters went into action crying 'Jesus and no quarter!' Their prayer was apparently heard, but not in the way they might have wished. They were mercilessly slaughtered by their Royalist opponents under the Marquess of Montrose, who claimed 'men might have walked upon dead corps to the town'. Between 1,300 and 2,000 Covenanters were slain.

1645

SCORCHED EARTH SMELLS SWEET IN THE NOSTRILS OF THE LORD

Dunnottar Castle, held by the Covenanters under William Keith, 7th Earl Marischal, was besieged by a Royalist force under the Marquess of Montrose. As the latter burnt the adjacent Keith lands, which were 'utelrie spoilzeit, plunderit and undone', a Presbyterian minister in the castle assured the Earl that 'the reek will be a sweet-smelling incense in the nostrils of the Lord'.

1649

BESSIE GRAHAM CONVERSES WITH THE FOUL FIEND

One Bessie Graham, a poor woman from Kilwinning, had used some harsh words against a neighbour who had subsequently died. Bessie was thrown into prison on suspicion of witchcraft, a charge she denied. The local minister, James Fergusson, was sent to examine her, and was inclined to think her innocent. Until, that is, he went to the prison one evening. Fergusson picks up the story:

> When I came to the stair-head, I resolved to halt a little to hear what she would say. Within a very short space, she begins to discourse, as if it had been to somebody with her. Her voice was so low, that I could not understand what she said, except one sentence, whereby I perceived she was speaking of somewhat I had been challenging her of and she had denied. After a little while, I heard another voice speaking and whispering as it were conferring with her, which presently I apprehended to be the Foul Fiend's voice. She, having kept silence a time, began to speak again; and before she had well ended, the other voice speaketh as it were a long sentence, which, though I understood not what it was, yet it was so low and ghostly, that I was certainly persuaded that it was another voice than hers. Besides, her accent and manner of speaking was as if she had been speaking to some other; and that other voice, to the best of my remembrance, did begin before she had ended, so that two voices were to be heard at once.

This testimony was sufficient to see Bessie condemned and executed.

BANDIT CHIEF SHOT IN EAR
WITH SILVER BULLET

At this time Caithness was being terrorised by a band of caterans led by a certain MacAllister. For some reason the bandit chief took a particular exception to the people of Thurso, who he imagined had given him some slight, and to avenge himself he decided to burn them all while they were in church. But news broke out of his intent, and the people determined to guard the seven doors of the kirk, to stop them being blockaded from the outside. An old woman wedged her prayer stool to keep one door open, while another door was defended by Sir James Sinclair of Murkle, who always came armed to Sunday service. When MacAllister tried to make entry, Sir James ran him through with his sword. This had no apparent effect, and so Sir James's servant, believing MacAllister must be invulnerable to cold steel, snipped a silver button from the jacket of his master, loaded it into his pistol, and discharged it at the bandit chief. MacAllister fell, muttering (in Gaelic) words to the effect that, 'Hoot toot! The bodach [old man] has deafened me.' He had been fatally shot in the ear. This cheered the congregation no end, who fell on their attackers and overwhelmed them.

1650

NAILING OF LUGS AND BORING OF TONGUES

In a diary entry for February, John Nicholl noted that lying and deception were on the up amongst the population:

> Much falset and cheating was detected at this time by the Lords of Session; for the whilk there was daily hanging, scourging, nailing of lugs [ears] and binding of people to the Tron [the public weighing-machine in Edinburgh], and boring of tongues; so that it was ane fatal year for false notars and witnesses, as daily experience did witness.

LADY BEATS GENERAL WITH LEG OF MUTTON

After his capture in Sutherland, the Royalist Marquess of Montrose was escorted south to face trial in Edinburgh by a force commanded by Major General James Holborne of Menstrie. His captors did their best to humiliate the Marquess, dressing him in rags and mounting him on an old nag. En route, the party spent a night at Skibo Castle, where their hostess was the Dowager Lady Gray, herself an ardent Royalist. Lady Gray requested that Montrose, as the guest of highest rank, be sat next to her at dinner. Holborne refused, insisting that the Marquess sit between himself and another officer. Furious at this breach of etiquette, Lady Gray seized a leg of mutton from the table and launched an attack against the person of the general, all the while reminding him and his fellow officers that when they were guests under her roof they would accord with her wishes as far as the seating plan was concerned. The point was taken, the Marquess re-seated, and civility restored. Only temporarily, as it turned out. In Edinburgh Montrose was sentenced to death, and on 21 May he was hanged on a gibbet 30 feet high. Thereafter his body was butchered: his head was placed on a spike on the Tolbooth, and his limbs sent to adorn the gates of Glasgow, Perth, Stirling and Aberdeen.

BLOOD RAINS DOWN ON BUCCLEUCH ESTATES

On 28 May it was noted that 'there rained blood the space of three miles in the Earl of Buccleuch's bounds, near the English Border; whilk was verified in presence of the Committee of State'.

1652

BIRDS FALL FROM SKY, PEOPLE FALL TO THEIR KNEES

On the morning of 29 March, between eight and eleven o'clock, a total eclipse of the sun plunged much of Scotland into 'ane manifest darkness for the space of some moments'. The eclipse passed from the southwest to the northeast, spreading terror as it cut across the country. Birds fell from the sky, and likewise many people fell to their knees in prayer. 'The like, as thought by astrologers, was not since the darkness at our Lord's passion.' Work in the fields ceased, in the expectation that the End of the World had come. It hadn't, but the day was ever after remembered as 'Murk Monday'.

WITCHCRAFT ACCUSATIONS: 'MUCH MALICE AND LITTLE PROOF'

Cromwell appointed four English commissioners to administer justice in Scotland. Many cases were brought before them of persons who had confessed to crimes before the kirk rather than the civil authorities. Among these cases were two women accused of witchcraft, as reported by *Mercurius Politicus*, the semi-official newspaper of the Cromwellian regime:

The court demanding how they came to be proved witches, they declared they were forced to it by the exceeding torture they were put to, which was by tying their thumbs behind them, and then hanging them up by them: two Highlanders whipped them, after which they set lighted candles to the soles of their feet, and between their toes, then burned them by putting lighted candles in their mouths, and then burning them in the head: there were six of them accused in all, four whereof died of the torture . . . Another woman that was suspected, according to their thoughts, to be a witch, was twenty-eight days and nights with bread and water, being stripped stark naked, and laid upon a cold stone, with only a haircloth over her. Others had hair-shirts dipped in vinegar put on them, to fetch off the skin.

The commissioners resolved to put a stop to such cruelties, although further details of these particular cases are unknown. Another report of the time tells us that the commissioners had some 50 cases of alleged witchcraft brought before them, but 'they found so much malice and so little proof against them, that none were condemned'.

1653
HANGED PERSON FOUND TO BE BOTH MAN AND WOMAN

On 11 February a certain Margaret Rannie was hanged 'on account of some irregularities of conduct'. Margaret, it turned out, was 'both man and woman, a thing not ordinar in this kingdom', and when her cadaver was handed over to the anatomists, she 'was found to be two every way, having two hearts, two livers, two every inward thing'.

SCOTLAND FOUND TO BE FULL OF WILD DISCONSOLATE HILLS

In London, James Howell published *A German Diet, or, the balance of Europe wherein the power and weakness . . . of all the kingdoms and states of Christendom are impartially poised, at a solemn convention of some German princes*. The book contains the following disobliging remarks about Scotland:

Good Lord, what a pitiful poor country is it! It were no petty kind of punishment to be banished thither, for it is a country only for those to dwell in that want a country, and have no part of the earth besides to dwell upon. In some parts the soil is such that it turns trees to stones, and wheat to oats; apples to crabs, and melons to pumpions [pumpkins]. In some places as you shall pass along, you shall see neither bird in the air, nor beast on the earth, nor worm creeping on the ground, nor scarce any vegetal, but black gorsy soil, a raw rheumatic air, or some scraggy and squalid wild disconsolate hills. And touching woods, groves and trees, as Stephen might have 'scaped stoning in Holland for want of stones, so if Judas had betrayed Christ in Scotland, he might (as one said) have repented before he could have found out a tree to have hanged himself upon.

A LANGUAGE WITH 11 DIFFERENT GENDERS

Sir Thomas Urquhart of Cromarty published *Logopandecteision*, a work dedicated 'To Nobody'. In this learned book Urquhart outlined an artificial language that he had created or intended to create. He claimed this language would be so simple that a ten-year-old could learn it in three months. Yet this language, he promised, would embrace 12 parts of speech, 11 genders, 11 cases, 11 tenses, seven moods, four numbers and four voices. In addition, it would contain words that could convey in seven syllables notions that other languages could only convey in 95 words. It is likely that Urquhart's intentions were satirical.

1654
CLAN CHIEF BITES OUT THROAT OF ENGLISH OFFICER

During a skirmish near Inverlochy with General Monck's troops, the Royalist clan chief Sir Ewen Cameron of Lochiel, found himself engaged in hand-to-hand combat with an English officer of great size and strength. Lochiel managed to knock his enemy's sword from his hand, but the man closed in on him and bore him to the ground, with his full weight upon him. As his would-be killer reached out for his sword, Lochiel grabbed the man's collar and, 'springing at his throat, seized it with his teeth, and gave so sure and effectual a bite that the officer died almost instantly'. 'This,' said Lochiel, 'was the sweetest bite I ever had in my life.'

MUSICIAN EATEN BY VERMIN

(4 September) A musician called Andrew Hill was put on trial, charged with abducting his pupil, Marion Foulis, daughter of Foulis of Ravelston. The ancillary charge that he had used sorcery to steal the young lady's affections was dismissed by the jury, although he was found guilty of abduction, and of being 'a foolish boaster of his skill in herbs and roots for captivating women'. His sentence was to be pronounced two weeks later, but in the interval he was 'eaten of vermin in prison, and so died'.

1656

WINE MIXED WITH MILK AND BRIMSTONE

Contemporaries complained about the adulteration of beverages practised by certain Edinburgh merchants. Wine was often mixed with milk and brimstone, while ale was made 'strong and heavy' by the addition of hemp seed, coriander seed, Turkish pepper, soot and salt.

1659

GOD DISPLEASED WITH TAX ON BEER

A tax of 8d. per pint was levied on beer in Edinburgh. The consequences were fearful, as described by the diarist John Nicoll:

> This imposition upon the ale and beer seemed not to thrive, for at the same instant, viz., upon the 1st, 2nd, 3rd and 4th days of September, God from the heavens declared His anger by sending thunder, fire and unheard tempest and storms and inundations of waters, which destroyed their common mills, dams and works, to the Town's great charges and expense.

LORD FAKES OWN DEATH BY DROWNING

To the astonishment of many, Lord Belhaven returned to Scotland, having been thought to be dead some five or six years. In fact, having fallen badly into debt, he had fled from his creditors to England, arranging that his servant should take back his cloak and hat to his wife, along with the tragic news that he had drowned in the treacherous quicksands of the Solway Firth. Only his wife and servant knew the truth. Once in England, Belhaven disguised himself as a gardener, and hired himself out as such. Eventually, his debts having been settled, he felt safe enough to return to Scotland to 'resume his rank'. However, while he was away his only son and heir died of a fever. 'In this real death by God's hand, who will not be mocked,' observed the Reverend William Baillie, 'the hope of that house perished.'

THE YOUTH WITH THE DEXTEROUS TOES

On 21 September John Nicoll reported in his diary that he had seen the most remarkable young man, a youth of 16 from Aberdeen, who had no power in his arms or hands, but who more than made up for this by the agility of his legs, feet and toes. He could write as swiftly and legibly as any notary, make his own pens, comb his hair, dress himself and thread a needle, 'in such short time and space as any other person whatsomever was able to do with his hands'.

1660

TEA LEAVES FOUND UNSUITABLE FOR GARNISHING BEEF

A London merchant, Thomas Garway, offered a new luxury good, selling at an astonishing £10 per pound: tea. Sir Walter Scott relates in 'The Life and Works of John Home' (*Quarterly Review*, June 1827) how this valuable stuff was first received in Scotland:

> The Scottish manners were, indeed, emerging from the Egyptian darkness of the preceding age, when a dame of no small quality, the worshipful Lady Pumphraston, buttered a pound of green tea sent her as an exquisite delicacy, dressed it as a condiment to a rump of salted beef, and complained that no degree of boiling would render these foreign greens tender.

1661

KING MIRACULOUSLY RESTORES
PLENTY TO THE NATION

The *Mercurius Caledonius*, an organ of Royalist propaganda, noted how much better things had become since the Restoration of Charles II. The fishing grounds along the east coast, the paper reported, had been so barren since the king had been in exile, 'that the poor men who subsisted by the trade, were reduced to go a-begging in the in-country. But now, blessed be God, since his majesty's return, the seas are so plentiful, that in some places they are in a condition to dung the land with soles.' What was more, the *Mercurius* claimed, the swans that had deserted Linlithgow Loch, and the fish called 'the Cherry of Tay', that had gone into exile with the king, had returned to their native waters.

The Presbyterian clergy took a different view. 'Nothing to be seen but debauch and revelling,' one minister muttered, 'nothing heard but clamorous crimes, all flesh corrupted their way . . . They made the church their stews [brothel]; you might have found chambers filled with naked men and women; cursing, swearing, and blasphemy were as common as prayer and worship was rare.'

PREGNANT ALE-WIVES RACE UP ARTHUR'S SEAT

The *Mercurius Caledonius* reported that a dozen pregnant ale-wives had raced up Arthur's Seat in Edinburgh 'for a groaning cheese of one hundred pound weight'. The second prize was 'a budgell of Dunkeld aquavitae'. The following day, the paper announced, 'sixteen fish-wives to trot from Musselburgh to the Canon Cross for twelve pair of lamb's harrigals [viscera]'.

BLOOD STILL DRIPS FROM LONG-SEVERED HEAD

The ardent Presbyterian minister James Guthrie was tried for treason before Parliament, the main charge being that he had rejected the king's authority over the kirk. The commissioner presiding over these proceedings was General John Middleton, who had joined Charles II on his return to Scotland in 1650, and whom Guthrie had shortly thereafter excommunicated, despite the pleas of the General Assembly. Guthrie was hanged on 1 June 1661, and his head displayed on the Nether Bow Port. In *The History of the Sufferings of the Church of Scotland from the Restoration to the Revolution* (1721–2), Robert Wodrow recounts that a few months after Guthrie's execution General Middleton was riding under the Nether Bow Port in a coach when a considerable number of drops of blood fell on the roof of the coach from Guthrie's severed head. The resulting stain could not, however hard the servants scrubbed at it, be removed.

SCOTSWOMEN: UNCLEANLY AND SLUTTISH

The noted English naturalist John Ray visited Scotland, of which he had no great opinion, as he recorded in his *Itineraries*:

> The women, generally, to us seemed none of the handsomest. They are not very cleanly in their houses, and but sluttish in dressing their meat. . . . The Scots cannot endure to hear their country or countrymen spoken against. They have neither good bread, cheese, or drink. They cannot make them, nor will they learn. Their butter is very indifferent, and one would wonder how they could contrive to make it so bad. . . . The people seem to be very lazy, at least the men . . .

1662

BLEEDING CORPSE PROVES GUILT

A maltman from Kirkcaldy called Grieve was found murdered. Suspicion fell on his son, as the two had quarrelled. The son denied he had had any hand in his father's death. But when he was brought into the presence of his father's corpse, and told to take his father's hand in his, the corpse bled from the nose. This did not happen when the dead man's wife touched the corpse. This proof of the son's guilt being established, the young man confessed, and was hanged.

STONE FOUND IN HEART OF DEAD BOY

(October 15) Death of Colin Lindsay, 2nd Earl of Balcarres, aged only 12. While he was being prepared for embalming, 'in his heart was found a notched stone, the bigness of one's five fingers'. This was witnessed by a physician and an apothecary who were present.

1663

LIONESS SUCKLES LAMB

In March the diarist John Nicholl noted a curious example of inter-species adoption:

> There was ane lioness brought to Edinburgh with ane lamb in its company, with whom she did feed and live; wha did embrace the lamb in her arms, as gif it had been her awn birth.

1664

EARL DIES AFTER DRINKING SEA WATER

(15 July) Death of Alexander Leslie, 2nd Earl of Leven, 'of a high fever'. This apparently followed on from 'a large carouse with the Earl of Dundee at Edinburgh and the Queensferry'. Some said that the two, while crossing the Forth, toasted each other with sea water, which they followed, when they made landfall, with sack (sweet white wine). It was to this fateful combination that some attributed the death of the young Earl, who was only 26 or 27 when he died.

DUTCH GIN GALORE

The Dutch ship *Kennermerland* foundered on the rocky shores of the Out Skerries, Shetland. On board was a cargo of strong spirits. It was many weeks before the locals returned to sobriety.

1669

MAD BRIDE FOUND IN SHIFT DABBLED IN GORE

(24 August) The Honourable Janet Dalrymple, daughter of the first Lord Stair, married David Dunbar of Baldoon in Wigtonshire. The bridegroom was not of her choosing; Janet had earlier fallen in love with Lord Rutherford, who had reciprocated her feelings, and the two had plighted their troths. But Janet's forceful mother disapproved and had broken off the engagement in favour of Dunbar, despite the pleas of the rejected lover. The wedding went ahead, but throughout the proceedings 'the bride remained like one lost in a reverie, and who only moves and acts mechanically'. When it came time for the couple to retire, Dunbar locked the door of the bridal chamber. Robert Chambers picks up the story in his *Domestic Annals of Scotland*:

> . . . suddenly there was heard to proceed from the bridal-chamber a loud and piercing outcry, followed by dismal groans. On its being opened, the alarmed company found the bridegroom weltering in his blood on the threshold, and the bride cowering in a corner of the chimney, with no covering but her shift, and that dabbled in gore. She told them 'to take up their bonny bridegroom'. It was evident she was insane, and the general belief was that she had franticly stabbed her husband. From that moment, she made no other rational communications, but pined away and died in less than three weeks. Young Baldoon recovered, but would never enter into explanations regarding the tragic occurrence.

The story provided Sir Walter Scott with the basis of his 1819 novel, *The Bride of Lammermoor*.

SEA CAPTAIN SUFFERS BITTER HOMECOMING

A certain Grizzel Jaffrey was executed at the Sea-gate of Dundee for witchcraft. The very day of her death, according to local tradition, her only son, the master of a vessel, sailed into Dundee harbour after a long absence. When he heard that all the commotion about the town was in consequence of his mother's death, he immediately set sail once more, and was never again heard of in his native town.

1670

SCOTTISH AIR WHOLESOME BUT FOR STINKING PEOPLE THAT INHABIT IT

In London an anonymous pamphlet was published entitled *A Perfect Description of the People and Country of Scotland*. Among its many observations are the following:

> First, for the Countrey, I must confess it is good for those that possess it, and too bad for others, to be at the charge, to conquer it. The Air might be wholesome, but for the stinking people that inhabit it. The ground might be fruitful had they wit to manure it. Their beasts be generally small, women only excepted, of which sort there are none greater in the whole world. There is great store of Fowl, too, as foul houses, foul sheets, foul dishes and pots, foul trenchers and napkins ... For their Butter and Cheese, I will not speak withal at this time, nor no man else at any time that loves his life. They have great store of Deer, but they are so far from the place where I have been, that I had rather believe than go to disprove it: I confess, all the Deer I met withal, was dear Lodgings, dear Horse-meat, and dear Tobacco and English Beer. As for Fruit, for their Grandsire Adam's sake, they never planted any.

1671

THE WOMAN WITH THE UNICORN HORN

(14 May) A young woman called Elizabeth Low underwent an operation at the hands of Arthur Temple of Ravelrig to excise an 11-inch 'horn' growing from her forehead. The item was subsequently deposited in the museum of Edinburgh University. Some years later, in 1682, it was noted that the unfortunate woman had another horn growing in the same place.

1674

A PREMATURE BURIAL

In Chirnside, Berwickshire, the death occurred of Marjorie Halcrow Erskine. She was buried in a shallow grave by the sexton, who intended to return later to steal her jewellery. When he attempted to put this plan into effect by cutting off her finger to obtain a ring, the unfortunate woman recovered consciousness. She went on to give birth to two sons.

1677

SERVANT BURNED AS WITCH AFTER
COUNTING TO 59

A gentlewoman of Haddington, one Margaret Kirkwood, was found hanging in her own house one Sunday morning in June when the rest of the family returned from church. It had been noted that during the service one of the family's servants, Lizzy Mudie, had made something of a disturbance by loudly counting out the numbers beginning with 'One, two, three' and continuing till she reached 59, upon which she cried 'The turn is done!' This appears to have coincided with the approximate time of Mistress Kirkwood's self-destruction, and the fact that the deceased was aged 59 was taken as conclusive proof that Lizzy Mudie had had a hand in her death. Lizzy's person was examined, and witch-marks were duly found upon her body. Lizzy confessed, and was burnt, but not before denouncing six other persons as witches. These were in turn examined by the official witch-pricker, whose proceedings were witnessed by the notable criminal advocate, Sir John Lauder. 'I remained very dissatisfied with this way of trial, as most fallacious,' wrote Lauder, 'and the fellow could give me no account of the principles of his art, but seemed to be a drunken foolish rogue.'

1678

A PIOUS BEQUEST DIVERTED

A certain Thomas Moodie left 20,000 merks to the magistrates of Edinburgh to build a new church. The magistrates, however, declared they had 'no use for a church', and decided instead to build a new prison, to house the increasing numbers of people jailed for religious offences. The new tolbooth, in the West Port, duly bore the name and arms of its inadvertent benefactor.

1679

THE WHITE LADY OF CORSTORPHINE

(26 August) The famous Corstorphine Sycamore on Corstorphine Hill (now within the bounds of Edinburgh) witnessed a notorious crime, when the elderly James, Lord Forrester, owner of Corstorphine Castle, was murdered by his young mistress, Christian Nimmo, the beautiful if highly strung wife of an Edinburgh merchant. She had heard that Forrester had, while drunk, 'spoken of her opprobriously', and, blinded with fury, she rushed to Corstorphine to upbraid him. Forrester was later found run through with his own sword. She herself sought to take refuge in a garret of the castle, but had dropped a slipper, which betrayed her whereabouts. Christian said that Forrester, in a drunken fury, had rushed at her with his sword, which she had seized, and upon which he then inadvertently impaled himself. The court before which she was brought did not accept her plea of self-defence, and she was sentenced to die. Imprisoned in the Tolbooth, she managed to escape disguised as a man, but was recaptured. On 12 November she was brought to the Mercat Cross, dressed all in black. The crowd gasped as she drew aside a long black veil to expose her white neck to the executioner. It was said that after her beheading her ghost would, on nights of the full moon, haunt the paths around the Corstorphine Sycamore, dressed all in white and carrying a bloody sword.

1680

SCOTLAND'S FIRST SIGHT OF AN ELEPHANT

In November of this year Scotland was visited for the first time by an elephant. Robert Law's *Memorials* includes his impressions of this novelty:

> . . . a great beast, with a great body and a great head, small eyes and dull, lugs like two skates lying close to its head; having a large trunk coming down from the nether end of the forehead, of length a yard and a half, in the undermost part small, with a nostril; by which trunk it breathed and drank, casting up its meat and drink in its mouth below it; having two large and long bones or teeth, of a yard length, coming from the upper jaw of it, and at the far end of it inclining one to another, by which it digs the earth for roots . . . it was backed like a sow, the tail of it like a cow's; the legs were big, like pillars or great posts, and broad feet with toes like round lumps of flesh . . . It was taught to flourish the colours with the trunk of it, and to shoot a gun, and to bow the knees of it, and to make reverence with its big head. They also rode upon it. Let this great creature on earth and the whale at sea be compared with a midge or minnow, and behold what great wisdom and power is with the great God, the creator and preserver of both!

MEIKLE JOHN AND THE QUEEN OF SHEBA

Hearing of his imminent arrest, the preacher John Gibb (whom even the radical Covenanters regarded as a fanatic 'with demented and enthusiastical delusions'), fled to the moors between the Pentland Hills and Tweedale, convinced that the City of Edinburgh would soon be destroyed by fire and tempest. He and his two dozen followers rejected private property, earthly authority and manual labour, which they regarded as the Devil's work, and instead spent the time praying, fasting and chanting the Psalms with doleful voices – earning them the ironical nickname of 'the Sweet Singers'. Gibb, known as 'Meikle John', seems to have exerted a particular magnetism over the opposite sex, who comprised the vast majority of his following, and to whom he gave biblical names such as Deborah, Lidiah and the Queen of Sheba. When some of the husbands of these women turned up to reclaim their wives, Gibb repelled them at pistol point. Gibb's Kingdom did not last long, however. In May 1681 he and his followers were seized by government troops, and Gibb appears to have suffered a breakdown – or at least a rejection of his former 'disloyal principals'. The Duke of York, Charles II's viceroy in Scotland, declared that Gibb rather deserved bedlam than the gallows. Accordingly, he was transported to America, where he died around 1720.

1681

LORD CHANCELLOR ALWAYS EITHER DRUNK OR SICK

Death of John Leslie, Duke of Rothes, Lord Chancellor of Scotland. In his *History of My Own Time*, Bishop Gilbert Burnet gave the following verdict on His Grace:

> He delivered himself without either restraint or decency to all the pleasures of wine and women. He had but one maxim, to which he adhered firmly, that he was to do everything, and deny himself in nothing, that might maintain his greatness, or gratify his appetites.

'The Duke of Rothes,' Burnet continues, 'was unhappily made for drunkenness.' He not only got himself drunk, but was also the cause of drunkenness in others, who were less able to take hard drink than he himself:

> This had a terrible conclusion; for, after he had killed all his friends, he fell at last under such a weakness of stomach that he had perpetual colics, when he was not hot within and full of strong liquor, of which he was presently seized; so that he was always either drunk or sick.

He died, without male heir, of jaundice, and with him the dukedom was extinguished.

1682

HANGMAN HANGED

(16 January) A certain Alexander Cockburn was put on trial for the murder in his own house in Edinburgh of a Bluegown (licensed) beggar called Adamson. The evidence was largely circumstantial: although others swore that it was so, Cockburn had denied that the beggar had been in his house the day of his death. However, on that day groans had been heard, and bloody clothes found in the house, and Cockburn was condemned to the gallows on the basis of this slender evidence. But as Cockburn was himself the hangman of Edinburgh, a substitute had to be found to carry out the office. The vacancy was gladly filled by one Mackenzie, whom, Sir John Lauder tells us, 'Cockburn had caused to lose his place of hangman at Stirling'.

VISCOUNTESS ADMINISTERS PUNNING PUT-DOWN

John Graham of Claverhouse, Viscount Dundee, nicknamed 'Bluidy Clavers', was appointed sheriff of Wigtonshire, in which capacity he carried on a ruthless persecution of the local Covenanters. A staunch Episcopalian, he often inveighed against John Knox, the great Presby-terian reformer of the previous century. This provoked the formidable Margaret Dalrymple, Viscountess Stair, to make the following rebuke. 'Why are you so severe on the character of John Knox?' she asked him. 'You are both reformers: he gained his point by clavers [talk]; you attempt to gain yours by knocks.' When she died in 1692, Viscountess Stair 'desired that she might not be put under ground, but that her coffin should stand upright on one end of it, promising that, while she remained in that situation, the Dalrymples should continue to flourish'. This unorthodox request confirmed the opinion of many that she was in league with the Devil.

DOG FOUND GUILTY OF TREASON

The Test Acts of 1673 and 1678 – which were designed to exclude Catholics and Non-conformists (such as Presbyterians) from public office – were long subject to ridicule. In 1682 the boys of Heriot's Hospital in Edinburgh decided that the dog that guarded their school-yard was the holder of a public office, and must therefore be subject to the Test. So they offered him the paper on which the required oath was written. Sir John Lauder, the contemporary chronicler, picks up the story:

> But he, loving a bone better than it, absolutely refused it. They then rubbed it over with butter, which they called an Explication of the Test . . . and he licked off the butter, but did spit out the paper; for which they held a jury upon him, and . . . they found the dog guilty of treason, and actually hanged him.

1683
MINISTER DRESSES IN UNDERGARMENTS OF HIS BELOVED

John McQueen, a minister in Edinburgh, became besotted with a Mrs Euphame Scott. She, however, treated him with disdain. In pursuance of his suit, McQueen somehow got hold of 'one of her undergarments, out of which he made a waistcoat and pair of drawers, by wearing which he believed the lady would infallibly be induced to give him her affections'. This turned out not to be the case, and McQueen was temporarily suspended from his clerical duties.

1684
A TAILOR TRIMMED

James Gavin, a tailor in the village of Douglas, suffered a severe punishment for his Covenanting beliefs. He had his ears cut off with his own scissors, and was subsequently transported to work in the plantations of the West Indies.

DEATH ON STAGE

A German quack doctor called Cornelius Tilberg (or Tilborg, or Tilbury, or à Tilbourne) was granted a licence to erect a stage in Edinburgh to demonstrate his skills. He had conducted demonstrations in London before the king in which physicians had dosed him with various poisons, whose deleterious effects he counteracted by the consumption of considerable quantities of oil. However, when he repeated the experiment in Edinburgh upon his manservant, the unfortunate subject died.

KING WILLIAM TRIES ON THE THUMBIKINS

A new instrument of torture was introduced to Scotland by the Privy Council, at the recommendation of General Tam Dalyell (aka Bluidy Tam, aka the Muscovy Beast), who had witnessed its efficacy while serving in Russia. This was the thumbikins – a device we now know as the thumbscrew. One of the first persons to suffer the thumbikins was William Spence, an agent of the Earl of Argyll. For some weeks Spence had been subjected to various tortures to persuade him to reveal what he knew of the rebellious plans of his master. Although kept awake for five nights in a row, and subjected to the Scotch Boot (a device that crushes the shin bone), Spence had kept firm. But after suffering the exquisite pain of having his thumbs crushed, Spence's resistance evaporated.

Another victim was the Whig politician William Carstairs, who was subjected to the thumbikins before the Privy Council. After the Glorious Revolution, Carstairs became an important adviser to William of Orange. With his star in the ascendant, Carstairs was presented by the Privy Council with the very thumbikins with which he had been tortured. After King William enquired what sort of instrument it was, Carstairs brought the thumbikens to their next meeting. 'I must try it,' said the king; 'I must put in my thumbs here. Now, Carstairs, turn the screw. Oh not so gently – another turn – another. Stop, stop! No more! Another turn, I am afraid, would make me confess anything.'

1685

SATAN'S INVISIBLE WORLD DISCOVERED

George Sinclair, mathematician, engineer and professor of philosophy at the University of Glasgow, published *Satan's Invisible World Discovered, or, A Choice Collection of Modern Relations, proving evidently against the Saducees and Atheists of this present age, that there are Devils, Spirits, Witches, and Apparitions, from Authentick Records, Attestations of Famous Witnesses, and undoubted Verity*. Among other things, Sinclair speculates on the origin of the 'second sight', a faculty supposed to be particularly common among the Highlanders:

I am undoubtedly informed, that men and women in the Highlands can discern fatality approaching others, by seeing them in waters, or with winding sheets about them . . . It is not improbable, but that such preternatural knowledge comes first by a compact with the Devil, and is derived downward by succession to their posterity, many of such I suppose are innocent, and have this sight against their will and inclination.

In discussing the fate of the so-called Witch of Lauder, who was executed in 1649, Sinclair demonstrates how impossible it was to escape the Satanic Dispensation. Just before she was to die, she made an announcement to the crowd, as recorded by Sinclair:

Now all you that did see me this day know that I am now to die as a witch by my own confession, and I free all men, especially the ministers and magistrates, of the guilt of my blood. I take it wholly upon myself: my blood be upon my own head. And as I must make answer to the God of Heaven presently, I declare that I am as free of witchcraft as any child: but being delated by a malicious woman, and put in prison under that name of a witch, disowned by my husband and friends, and seeing no ground of hope of my coming out of prison nor ever coming in credit again, through the temptation of the Devil I made up that confession on purpose to destroy my own life, being weary of it, and choosing rather to die than to live.

Sinclair draws the obvious conclusion:

Which lamentable story, as it did then astonish all the spectators, none of which could restrain themselves from tears, so it may be to all a demonstration of Satan's subtlety, whose design is to destroy all, partly by tempting many to presumption, and some others to despair.

DEAD FOR A DOG

Walking down the High Street of Edinburgh one day, the Hon. George Douglas recognised one of his family's dogs, which had been stolen from the house of his father, the Earl of Morton, shortly before. The dog was following the Laird of Chatto, whom Douglas accosted, informing him of the animal's ownership. Chatto happily surrendered the dog to its rightful owner, but some days later, as Douglas walked through the town with the dog at his heels, a footman of Chatto's called John Corsehill attempted to seize the animal. Douglas's complaint was met with a tirade of abuse. Insults were exchanged, each calling the other a rascal, and as Douglas attempted to draw his sword Corsehill struck him twice on the head with his cudgel. The assault continued, and Douglas attempted to parry the blows. But, a contemporary tells us, 'the footman was so furious, that he run himself upon the point of the sword, and so was killed'. It appears that Douglas's plea of self-defence, and that 'no gentleman could endure publicly to be called a rascal without resentment', was accepted.

DEVIL HURLS TABLE AT BLUIDY TAM

Death of General Tam Dalyell, aka Bluidy Tam, scourge of the Covenanters. His enemies told how Dalyell had been playing cards with the Devil one night at the Binns, his ancestral home. Such was Dalyell's cunning that he succeeded in outsmarting the Prince of Darkness, who flew into a fury and hurled a marble table at his opponent. It missed its mark, but carried on through the window before landing in Sergeant's Pond. The table is now back in the house, having been retrieved from the pond in 1878. As for the Devil, he threatened to blow down Dalyell's house, prompting Dalyell to declare that 'I will build me a turret at every corner to pin down my walls.'

1686

THE GHOSTLY ARMIES OF CLYDE

In his memoirs (published as *Biographia Presbyteriana* in 1827), the Covenanting rebel Patrick Walker recalls visions seen by many in the Clyde Valley:

In the year 1686, especially in the months of June and July, about Crossford-boat, two miles below Lanark, especially at the Mains on the Water of Clyde, many people gathered together for several afternoons, where there were showers of bonnets, hats, guns, and swords, which covered the trees and ground; companies of men in arms marching along the water-side; companies meeting companies all through other, and then all falling to the ground, and disappearing, and other companies appearing the same way. I went there three after-noons together, and, as I could observe, there were two of the people that were together saw, and a *third that saw not*; and *though I could see nothing*, yet there was such a fright and trembling upon those that did see, that was discernible to all from those that saw not. There was a gentleman standing next to me who spoke as too many gentlemen and others speak. He said: 'A pack of damned witches and warlocks that have the second-sight! De'il haet do I see!' And immediately there was a discernible change in his countenance, with as much fear and trembling as any woman I saw there; who cried out: 'Oh, all ye that do not see, say nothing; for I persuade you it is matter of fact, and discernible to all that is not stone-blind!' Those that did see, told what works the guns had, and their length and wideness; and what handles the swords had, whether small, or three-barred, or Highland guards; and the closing knots of the bonnets, black and blue; and these who did see them there, wherever they went abroad, saw a bonnet and a sword drop in the way. I have been at a loss ever since, what to make of this last. However a profane age may mock, disdain and make sport of these extraordinary things, yet these are no new things, but some such things have been in former times . . .

SKIPPER THROWN OVERBOARD FOR SMOKING

Around this time, Andrew Fletcher of Saltoun was in political exile in the Netherlands. Mrs Calderwood of Polton met him there on her travels, and told a story about the irascible Scottish patriot, who, she said, 'could not endure the smoke of toback'. Finding himself aboard a Dutch ship whose master would not desist from smoking, he sought relief on deck.

The skipper was so contentious that he followed him, and on whatever side Saltoun sat, he put his pipe in the cheek next him, and whiffed in his face. Saltoun went down several times and brought up stones in his pocket from the ballast, and slipped them into the skipper's pocket that was next the water, and when he found he had loadened him as much as would sink him, he gives him a shove, so that over he hirsled [i.e. slithered overboard]. The boat went on, and Saltoun came down among the rest of the passengers, who probably were asleep, and fell asleep among the rest. In a little time, bump came the scoot [boat] against the side, on which they all damned the skipper but, behold, when they called, there was no skipper; which would breed no great amazement in a Dutch company.

Another story about Fletcher concerns his footman. The latter, tired of his master's rages, handed in his notice. 'Why do you desire to leave my service?' Fletcher asked.

'Because, sir, to tell the truth, I cannot bear your temper,' the man said.

'To be sure,' Fletcher replied, 'I am passionate, but my anger is no sooner on than it's off.'

'Aye, that's true, sir, but it's no sooner off than it's on again.'

1688

BAN ON THE EXPORT OF HAIR

With the fashion for lavish periwigs with curls cascading down over the shoulders, there was a huge demand among foreign wig-makers for human hair. There were reports that some Scottish women had come to an arrangement with travelling merchants to harvest their heads at regular intervals, at a charge of a guinea a crop. As a consequence of such activities, the wig-makers of Scotland complained to the Privy Council that there was no Scottish hair to be had to supply the native industry. In response, in January 1688 the Privy Council issued an edict against the export of hair.

CORPSE BLEEDS ON SON'S HANDS

Sir James Stanfield, an English manufacturer who had set up business in East Lothian, was found dead in a pool of water near his house at New Mills. It was known that he had suffered from melancholy, perhaps as a result of domestic unhappiness – he had recently disin-herited his son Patrick, whom he had accused of profligacy. Both Patrick and Sir James's widow asserted that Sir James had taken his own life, and hastened to bury him. However, suspicions were aroused, not least by the haste of the burial. An exhumation was ordered, and the corpse examined by two surgeons from Edinburgh. The surgeons made an incision in the neck, and thereby established (to their own satisfaction at least) that death had been by strangulation. The incision having been sewn up and the body washed and put in clean linen, the corpse was carried to its coffin by James Row, an Edinburgh merchant, on one side, and Patrick Stanfield on the other. Those present were shocked when the corpse began to bleed copiously on Patrick's side, staining his hands with blood. Horrified, Patrick cried to God for mercy, and collapsed on the ground groaning. This was taken as proof of his guilt, and he was sent to trial on 7 February 1688. Little further evidence was offered, apart from the fact that Patrick had cursed his father, but this was enough to find him guilty. He was hanged on 24 February, but the rope slipped and Patrick ended up on his knees. The hangmen finished the botched job by means of strangulation, after which Patrick's tongue was cut out as punishment for having cursed his father, and his hand amputated and placed on the East Port of Haddington. The body was suspended in chains, but was secretly removed and later found in a ditch. The pious pointed out the hand of Providence in the fact that the son had, like the father, been strangled, and his corpse found in a pool of water.

MUSICIAN NAILED TO PILLORY BY HIS EAR

In Inverness, a musician called Niven had persuaded a minister to marry him to his 12-year-old pupil by recruiting a youth to impersonate the girl's brother and to convey the apparent permission of the girl's father, also a minister. This 'abominable imposture and treachery' resulted in Niven being nailed to the pillory by his ear. He was subsequently banished.

PUPPIES HANGED ON DOCTRINAL GROUNDS

In Aberdeen, Peter Gibbs, the father of the architect James Gibbs and a devout Roman Catholic, named his two young dogs Calvin and Luther, the two pillars of the Protestant faith. The local magistrates took umbrage, and ordered the innocent puppies to be hanged at the Cross 'as a terror to evil-doers'.

1689

VIOLENT REACTION TO CHILD SUPPORT RULING

John Chiesley of Dalry was incensed when Sir George Lockhart, President of the Court of Session, ruled that he should pay 'an alimentary provision of about £93 in favour of his wife and child'. Nursing his grievance, Chiesley pursued the judge with a hidden pistol, first intending to assassinate him in church, 'but was diverted by some feeling concerning the sanctity of the place'. At the end of the service he trailed Sir George up the Lawnmarket, and shot him dead outside his own house. The assassin would not flee, instead proclaiming, 'I have taught the President how to do justice.' The authorities took a dim view of both deed and claim, and Chiesley was tried before the Lord Provost of Edinburgh. The latter handed down an exemplary sentence, which was carried out on 3 April. The guilty man was dragged on a hurdle to the place of execution, where his right hand was struck off while he still lived. He was then hanged on the gallows with the offending pistol tied round his neck.

THE HANDKERCHIEF SPY

Following the Glorious Revolution, supporters of the exiled James II held Edinburgh Castle. Several Edinburgh citizens were confined in the Tolbooth, accused of signalling to the besieged garrison. One of those imprisoned, Alexander Ormiston, had been arrested for waving his handkerchief as he walked through the Grassmarket. However, he claimed that he had merely been wiping his eyes, which had caused him irritation and pain since infancy. He obtained his release after 12 days.

THE COLONEL WHO WOULD NOT BE BURIED

While government troops burnt his castle at Inverey in Deeside, the hot-tempered Jacobite Colonel John Farquharson was obliged to take refuge in 'the Colonel's Bed' – a rocky ledge in the depths of the gorge of the Ey Burn. Here his mistress Annie Ban, the great love of his life, brought him food. Before his death in around 1698 Farquharson had left instructions that he should be buried beside Annie Ban at Inverey. However, his wishes were ignored, and he was buried at Braemar. The next morning his coffin was seen to have found its way back to the surface of the earth. It was re-buried, but reappeared, re-buried again, and reappeared again. Having thus made his wishes abundantly clear, Farquharson was duly interred as he had requested, beside his beloved Annie Ban at Inverey.

1690

TORTURE JUDGED CONSISTENT WITH HUMANITY

Henry Neville Payne, an English Catholic agent of the exiled King James, was arrested in Dumfriesshire and taken to Edinburgh, where in December the Privy Council put him to the torture – despite the fact that the Declaration or Claim of Rights had declared torture unlawful. The Earl of Crawford presided over the interrogation of Payne, which involved the application of both thumbscrews and the boot. Crawford left an account of the proceedings:

About six this evening, we inflicted [the torture] on both thumbs and one of his legs, with *all the severity that was consistent with humanity,* even unto that pitch that *we could not preserve life and have gone further,* but without the least success. He was so manly and resolute under his suffering, that such of the Council as were not acquainted with all the evidences, were brangled and began to give him charity, that he might be innocent. It was surprising to me and others, that flesh and blood could, without fainting, and in contradiction to the grounds we had insinuat of our knowledge of his accession in matters, *endure the heavy penance he was in for two hours.* My stomach is truly so far out of tune, by being a witness to an act so far cross to my natural temper, that I am fitter for rest than anything else.

Again in contradiction of the Claim of Rights, Payne was kept in prison without trial for many years, and was not released until 1701.

1691
THE COUNTRY'S GONE TO THE DOGS – AGAIN

The General Assembly, in declaring a national fast to be held on the second Thursday of January, bemoaned the moral state of Scotland:

There hath been a great neglect of the worship of God in public, but especially in families and in secret. The wonted care of sanctifying the Lord's day is gone . . . [The] cities full of violence . . . so that blood touched blood. Yea, Sodom's sins have abounded amongst us, pride, fullness of blood, idleness, vanities of apparel, and shameful sensuality . . . Few are turned to the Lord; the wicked go on doing wickedly, and there is found among us to this day shameful ingratitude for our mercies [and] horrid impenitency under our sins . . . There is great want of piety towards God and love towards man, with a woeful selfishness, everyone seeking their own things, few the public good or ane other's welfare

With a singular lack of self-awareness, the document ends by decrying the fact that the vast majority are 'more ready to censure the sins of others, than to repent of their own'.

1692
A PRAYER FOR FOOLS

A Mr Erskine was recorded in *Scotch Presbyterian Eloquence* as having offered up the following prayer in Edinburgh's Tron Church:

> Lord, have mercy on all fools and idiots, and particularly on the magistrates of Edinburgh.

1694
A DUPLICATING MACHINE

A man called James Young claimed to have invented 'ane engine for writing, whereby five copies may be done at the same time, which it is thought may prove not unuseful to the nation'. The Privy Council granted Young a 19-year patent on this device, but no more was heard of it.

1695
RUM BANNED AS A DANGEROUS DRUG

Parliament banned the sale of rum, as it competed with the domestic production of 'strong waters made of malt', i.e. whisky. Parliament also decreed that rum was 'rather a drug than a liquor, and highly prejudicial to the health of all who drink it'. Only eight years later, however, the Privy Council awarded certain merchants the right to establish a 'stillarie for distilling rum' in Leith, on the grounds that 'in this time of war, when commodities of that nature, how necessary soever, can hardly be got from abroad', such an operation would be 'necessary and beneficial to the country, and for the general use and advantage of the lieges'.

1697

MIRACLES DENOUNCED AS PRANKS

(8 January) Death of Thomas Aikenhead, the last person in Britain to be executed for blasphemy. In 1696, while in his third year at Edinburgh University, Aikenhead (the son of an apothecary) was summoned before the Privy Council, accused of uttering religious opinions so heterodox as to be blasphemous, and sent for trial. The prosecution was conducted by the Lord Advocate, Sir James Stewart, and the charges against Aikenhead asserted that 'the prisoner had repeatedly maintained, in conversation, that theology was a rhapsody of ill-invented nonsense, patched up partly of the moral doctrines of philosophers, and partly of poetical fictions and extravagant chimeras'. Furthermore, the indictment continued, Aikenhead had 'ridiculed the holy scriptures, calling the Old Testament Ezra's fables', and had 'railed on Christ, saying, he had learned magic in Egypt, which enabled him to perform those pranks which were called miracles'. In addition, 'he called the New Testament the history of the imposter Christ . . . said Moses was the better artist and the better politician; and he preferred Mahomet to Christ'. What was more, he claimed that 'the Holy Scriptures were stuffed with such madness, nonsense, and contradictions, that he admired the stupidity of the world in being so long deluded by them'. Finally, he was said to have maintained that Christianity would 'be utterly extirpat' within 100 years or so.

Despite the fact that Aikenhead had made a full recantation before his trial, which took place on 23 December 1696, the Lord Advocate demanded that he 'ought to be punished with death . . . to the example and terror of others', Aikenhead having shaken off 'all fear of God' and vented 'wicked blasphemies against God and our Saviour Jesus Christ'. Aikenhead was found guilty and sentenced to hang, but appealed to the Privy Council, pleading his 'deplorable circumstances and tender years'. The Privy Council ruled that they would only offer him a reprieve if the Church interceded on his behalf. In a spirit of Christian charity, the General Assembly considered that only a 'vigorous execution' of the sentence could curtail 'the abounding of impiety and profanity in this land'. Following his public hanging, one minister declared that 'God was glorified by such ane awful & exemplary punishment'.

1699

SCOT INVENTS FIREPROOF WOOD

A cabinetmaker called Robert Logan claimed to have invented a new method of making cauldrons and kettles out of wood. What was unusual about his vessels was, he claimed, that they could 'abide the strongest fire', and so could be used for boiling water, cooking stews, etc. The Earl of Leven vouchsafed for Logan's invention, and the Privy Council awarded him a monopoly for 'two nineteen years'.

ON THE LIMITED SHELF-LIFE OF CHRISTIANITY

Publication in London of *Theologiae Christianae Principia Mathematica* by the Scottish mathematician John Craig. In this work, Craig used Newtonian fluxional calculus to deduce that belief in the Christian religion would finally disappear in AD 3153. Contemporary critics found his position 'scandalous and prophane', but David Hume thought that Craig had a point.

THE THRASHER THRASHED

(July) In Moffat, a schoolboy called John Douglas was so severely beaten by his teacher, one Robert Carmichael, that he died. Carmichael fled, but after a few weeks he was apprehended. In January of the following year he was put on trial in Edinburgh, and, being found guilty, was sentenced

> to be taken from the Tolbooth of Edinburgh by the hangman under a sure guard to the middle of the Lawn-market, and there lashed by seven severe stripes; then to be carried down to the Cross, and there severely lashed by six sharp stripes; and then to be carried to the Fountain Well, to be severely lashed by five stripes; and then to be carried back by the hangman to the Tolbooth. Like as, the Lords banish the said Mr Robert furth of this kingdom, never to return thereto under all highest pains.

The
EIGHTEENTH
Century

1700
TWO FORGING THOMASES

(February) A poor scholar called Thomas M'Gie, spotting that all the denominations of notes issued by the Bank of Scotland were printed in the same typeface, sought to enrich himself by adding a zero to the £5 note. 'But good providence discovered the villainy before he had done any great damage,' a contemporary recorded, 'and the rogue was forced to fly abroad.' Subsequently, the Bank used different typefaces for different denominations, 'so that it is not in the power of man to renew M'Gie's villainy'. This commentator underestimated the length to which villainy will go in the matter of forgery, however. For example in 2007 Thomas McAnea, who worked in a Print Link shop in Maryhill, Glasgow, was jailed for his part in forging Bank of Scotland £20 and £50 notes. His expertise was in creating convincing holograms and watermarks in the dud notes, earning him the nickname 'Hologram Tam'.

SILVER IN THEM THERE HILLS

Around this time, Sir John Areskine of Alva operated a number of silver mines in the Ochil Hills, with mixed success. When accompanying a friend over his lands, he is reported to have pointed at one excavation and told his visitor, 'Out of that hole I took fifty thousand pounds.' Walking on, he pointed out another hole. 'And I put it all into *that* one.'

1702
DIVINE WRATH EXPLODES IN LEITH

(3 July) 'The distressed inhabitants of Leith' petitioned the Privy Council for relief after their town had been struck by calamity – one they admitted had been entirely deserved:

> It pleased the great and holy God to visit this town, for their heinous sins against him, with a very terrible and sudden stroke, which was occasioned by the firing of thirty-three barrels of powder; which dreadful blast, as it was heard even

at many miles distance with great tenor and amazement, so it hath caused great ruin and desolation in this place.

The deaths of seven or eight people, and the damage to many buildings, appears to have expiated the relevant sins, for 'the merciful conduct of Divine Providence hath been very admirable in the preservation of hundreds of people, whose lives were exposed to manifold sudden dangers'.

COCKING PROPOSED AS AN ALTERNATIVE TO WAR

Perhaps one of the sins that had offended the Almighty was the recent establishment on Leith Links of a cockpit, where punters paid 10d. for a front-row seat, 7d. for the second row, and 4d. for the third. Cock-fighting was at this time a novelty in Scotland, having been introduced by a fencing master called William Machrie, who insisted it was 'an art in vogue all over Europe', though 'kept up only by people of rank, and never sunk down to the hands of the commonalty'. Soon, however, 'the passion for cock-fighting was so general among all ranks of the people, that the magistrates discharged its being practised on the streets, on account of the disturbances it occasioned'. Machrie himself leapt to the defence of his sport, penning a pamphlet entitled *An Essay on the Innocent and Royal Recreation and Art of Cocking*. He would hear no ill of his favourite bird, praising 'his Spanish gait, his Florentine policy, and his Scottish valour', while reminding his readers that the cock had been 'an early preacher of repentance, even convincing Peter, the first pope, of his holiness's fallibility'. Although we think of cock-fighting as a bloody and inhumane sport, Mauchrie thought that it could become a substitute for war, and so relieve humanity of much suffering. Referring to the gentlemen who had established the cockpit at Leith Links, he says:

> I earnestly wish that their generous and laudable example may be imitated in that degree that, in cock-war, village may be engaged against village, city against city, kingdom against kingdom, nay, the father against the son, until all the wars in Europe, wherein so much Christian blood is spilt, be turned into the innocent pastime of cocking.

1705

WOMAN LYNCHED IN PITTENWEEM

(30 January) Janet Cornfoot, a woman from Pittenweem, was accused by a local fisherman, one Alexander Macgregor, of assaulting him in his bed, in the company of two other women and the Devil. Under torture she confessed to the crime, but subsequently retracted her confession. The local minister was inclined to believe her innocent, and helped her to escape, but she was apprehended by the minister of a neighbouring parish and returned to Pittenweem. There she was attacked by an angry mob, beaten, dragged through the streets and tied to a rope slung between a ship and the shore. Swinging on the rope she was pelted with stones until the crowd grew bored and dropped her to the ground. Here she was subjected to another beating, then pressed to death by a door weighted with rocks.

BOOK BURNING

(August) As the debate about a possible Union with England heated up, the Parliament in Edinburgh ordered that a book by one William Atwood be burnt by the hangman at the Cross. The offence Atwood had caused is summed up in his title: *The Superiority and Direct Dominion of the Imperial Crown of England over the Crown and Kingdom of Scotland.* On the same day that Parliament ordered the destruction of Atwood's book, it awarded £4,800 to a James Anderson, who had published a book with an altogether more obliging title, namely *A Historical Essay shewing that the Crown and Kingdom of Scotland is Imperial and Independent.*

WHYSHOULDITBETHOUG TATHINGINCREDI AND OTHER TYPOS

A duodecimo edition of the Bible was printed by a Mrs Anderson, who had inherited her husband's monopoly on the printing of the Scriptures in Scotland. Mrs Anderson apparently saw no need to employ a proofreader. The result was that her Bibles were full of virtually incomprehensible passages, such as the following: 'Whyshoulditbethoug tathingincredi File wtyou, it God should raise the dead?' Nevertheless, after the expiry of her monopoly, she was appointed by the Church of Scotland to be their official printer –

possibly because she had offered to buy up a vast quantity of the kirk's unsold stock of *Acts of the General Assembly*.

1707

MAN SHOT ATTEMPTING TO DEFEND HIS MARE'S HONOUR

David Ogilvie of Clunie, a noted young roisterer, took the opportunity of a funeral wake in the village of Meigle to get himself exceedingly drunk. He insisted on accompanying some of the other gentlemen home, although his own lay in another direction. During the course of the journey he caused great offence to one of his companions, Andrew Cowpar of Dunblair, 'by practical jokes of a gross kind, founded on the variance of sex in their respective horses'. To defend his mare's honour, Cowpar flicked his whip across the face of Ogilvie's stallion. Ogilvie took extreme umbrage, demanded Cowpar's whip, and, this being refused, he drew his pistol and shot the other man dead. Ogilvie evaded justice by fleeing abroad.

ROARING WHALES TERRORIZE FIFE AND THE LOTHIANS

(26 April) A school of pilot whales entered the Firth of Forth, 'roaring, plunging, and threshing upon one another, to the great terror of all who heard the same'. Thirty-five of the unfortunate creatures beached themselves at Kirkcaldy, 'where they made a yet more dreadful roaring and tossing when they found themselves aground, insomuch that the earth trembled'. An observer was troubled by this event, writing, 'What the unusual appearance of so great a number of them at this juncture of the union of the kingdoms may portend shall not be our business to inquire.'

CANNIBALISTIC IDIOT CELEBRATES THE UNION

James Douglas, Earl of Drumlanrig (1687–1715) was the eldest son of James Douglas, 2nd Duke of Queensberry, one of the leading figures behind the Union of 1707. James the Younger was, according to James Grant's *Old and New Edinburgh* (1880), 'an idiot of the most wretched kind, rabid and gluttonous as a wild animal'. This 'monstrous and unfortunate creature', who 'grew to an enormous stature' (as attested by the size of his leaden coffin in the family vault at Durisdeer), was kept confined by his father in a windowless ground-floor room in the west wing of Queensberry House in Edinburgh's Canongate – until one fateful day. Let Grant continue the story:

On the day the Treaty of Union was passed all Edinburgh crowded to the vicinity of the Parliament House to await the issue of the final debate, and the whole household of the Duke – the High Commissioner – went thither en masse for that purpose, and perhaps to prevent him from being torn to pieces by the exasperated people, and among them went the valet whose duty it was to watch and attend the Earl of Drumlanrig.

Hearing all unusually still in the vast house, the latter contrived to break out of his den, and roamed wildly from room to room till certain savoury odours drew him into the great kitchen, where a little turnspit sat quietly on a stool by the fire. He seized the boy, took the meat from the fire, stripped and spitted him, and he was found devouring the half-roasted body when the duke returned with his train from his political triumph, to find dire horror awaiting him. 'The common people, among whom the dreadful tale soon spread, in spite of the Duke's endeavours to suppress it, said that it was a judgment upon him for his odious share in the Union. The story runs that the Duke, who had previously regarded his dreadful offspring with no eye of affection, immediately ordered the creature to be smothered. But this is a mistake; the idiot is known to have died in England, and to have survived his father many years, though he did not succeed him upon his death in 1711, when the titles devolved upon Charles, a younger brother.'

Thereafter, the mad Earl was referred to by the Duke's anti-Union enemies as 'the Cannibalistic Idiot'. The oven he employed can still be viewed in the Allowances Office of the Scottish Parliament, of which Queensberry House now forms a part.

1709

THE GENTLEMAN VANISHES

(March) Sir Michael Balfour of Denmill in Fife, 'a quiet country gentleman', rode out early one morning with a servant 'to visit some friends and for other business'. Later that day the servant returned to Denmill Castle, reporting that Sir Michael had sent him on an errand to Cupar, and had told him that he would be home before him. But Sir Michael never returned home. His wife and children caused the entire neighbourhood to be searched, and enquiries were made in distant towns. Advertisements offering rewards were even placed in the newspapers of London and the capitals of Europe. To no avail.

Some said that Sir Michael, succumbing to melancholy, must have retired abroad, though there was nothing to suggest that the gentleman was anything but content. Others said he had orchestrated his own disappearance to avoid his debtors – but it seems Sir Michael owed little to anyone. The more fanciful suggested he had been 'transported and carried away by spirits'. The most popular theory was that, while riding at night, he must have fallen down a mineshaft. But all such pits that lay on his way home were searched, and no sign of either Sir Michael or his horse were ever found.

Many years later, in 1724, there appeared in a broadside the apparent confession of a woman who recalled that as a girl she had witnessed her parents fall upon and murder Sir Michael. He had called upon them to collect a debt, and while sitting at their fireside he had been run through with his own sword, then secretly buried alongside his horse. The tale turned out to be a fiction, and the mystery of the whereabouts of Balfour of Denmill has never been cleared up.

STIFFER FINES FOR GENTLEMEN FORNICATORS

(9 November) The proceedings of the Court of Session record this unusual defence:

> John Purdie, fined by the justices of the peace of Midcalder, in £100 Scots, for fornication with Christian Thomson, his servant, conformably to the last Act 38, Parl. 1661, he being the eldest son of an heritor [landowner], and so a *gentleman*,

in the construction of law; when charged for payment by Thomas Sandilands, collector of those fines, he suspended upon this ground, that the fine was exorbitant in so far that he was but a small heritor; and that the Act of Parliament imposeth the £100 upon *gentlemen transgressors*; and as all heritors are not gentlemen, *so he denied that he had the least pretence to the title of gentleman.* And farther, he had married the woman he offended with, which lessened the scandal, and was a ground to mitigate the fine. The lords sustained the reason of this suspension, to restrict the fine to £10 Scots; because *suspender had not the face or air of a gentleman.*

PUBLIC HUMILIATION AS A PASTORAL DUTY

The minister of Torryburn in Fife, the Revd Allan Logan, had the habit, while administering communion, of glancing along the pews until his eyes fell on some poor woman of whom he disapproved. He would then roar, 'You, witch-wife, get up from the table of the Lord.' The poor woman would then stand up and depart, perhaps believing that the minister had some inkling of her less pure thoughts. On one such occasion a woman called Helen Key, who had had enough of the Revd Logan's witch obsessions, turned to her neighbour, observed that the minister was 'daft', picked up her stool and left the kirk. For this she was hauled before the kirk session, convicted of profanity and obliged to sit before the congregation while her sins were publicly enumerated.

1712

FLEETS FIGHT IT OUT IN THE SKY

(May) Robert Wodrow reported that he had been told that the Laird of Waterside in Dumfriesshire and many others had witnessed an extraordinary spectacle in the sky at sunset near Penpont:

> There appeared to them, towards the sea, two large fleets of ship; near a hundred upon every side, and they met together and fairly engaged. They very clearly saw their masts, tackling, gun; and their firing one at another. They saw several of them

sunk; and after a considerable time's engagement they sundered, and one part of them went to the west and another to the south.

Around the same time, Wodrow received strange reports of 'shootings' from Kintyre:

> The people thought it had been thunder, and went out to see what sort of day it was like to be. All appeared clear, and nothing like thunder. There were several judicious people that saw, at some distance from them, several very great companies of soldiers marching with their colours flying and their drums beating, which they heard distinctly, and saw the men walking on the ground in good order; and yet there were no soldiers at all in that country, nor has been a long time. They heard likewise a very great shooting of cannon, so distinct and terrible, that many of the beasts broke the harrow and came running home.

ON THE BENEFITS OF BATHING IN ORDURE

Publication of *Tippermalloch's Receipts*, 'a medical vade-mecum of respectable families' by 'a worthy and ingenious gentleman', John Moncrieff of Tippermalloch, in Strathearn. The book was extensively consulted in the earlier years of the 18th century, and includes 'cures' that might have been condemned as witchcraft in the previous century if they had been administered by an old countrywoman. For 'cold distemper of the brain', Tippermalloch recommends that snails, bruised in their shells, should be applied to the forehead; for 'pestilential fever', a snail poultice should be applied to the soles of the feet; for 'decay of the hair', the head should be washed with the burnt ashes of dove's dung; for a well-coloured complexion, 'the liver of a sheep fresh and hot' should be applied to the face; for lethargy, the patient should take a powder prepared from the burnt skin, ears and nails of a hare; epilepsy might be prevented by wearing a girdle of wolf's hair, but if this fails, it can be treated by 'powder of a man's bones burnt, chiefly of the skull that is found in the earth . . . the bones of a man cure a man; the bones of a woman cure a woman'; deafness is to be cured by a mixture of ants' eggs and onion juice poured into the ear; haemorrhage may be stopped by pouring cow's blood into the wound; measles can be cured by intro-ducing a ewe into the chamber of the patient, the disease thus passing from the human to the animal, which then dies; and trapped wind is eased by taking a bath laced with the excreta of certain animals.

circa 1713
JACOBITES IN DRAG – PART I

Lady Euphemia, wife of the Jacobite spy Sir George Lockhart of Lee, used to visit Edinburgh dressed in male attire in order to pick up intel-ligence from the Whig coffee houses. On one occasion she learnt that an ardent Whig called Forbes had obtained some papers compromising her husband, and that he intended to forward these papers to the government. Daniel Wilson, in his *Reminiscences of Old Edinburgh*, describes what happened next:

> According to the narrative communicated to me by her nephew, Lady Euphemia Lockhart dressed her sons – two fair and somewhat effeminate-looking, though handsome youths, – in negligee, fardingale, and masks, with patches, jewels, and all the finery of accomplished courtesans. Thus equipped, they sallied out to the Cross, and watching for the Whig gallant, they soon won his favour, and inducing him to accompany them to a neighbouring tavern . . . [where] the pseudo fair ones fairly drank him below the table, and then rifled his pockets of the dangerous papers.

1714
CHEATING THE WORMS

Death of Sir Patrick Hume, the King's High Commissioner to Parlia-ment. Lord Binning, noting that Sir Patrick smiled upon his deathbed, asked the old man what amused him. 'I am diverted to think,' responded Sir Patrick, 'what a disappointment the worms will meet with when they bore through my thick coffin, expecting to find a good meal, and get nothing but the bones.'

COUNTESS THWARTED FROM DANCING ON HUSBAND'S GRAVE

Death of George, 1st Earl of Cromartie. He had left instructions that he was to be buried under a funerary obelisk raised upon a mound in the town of Dingwall, in order to thwart his wife's stated intention of dancing upon his grave.

1715

ROTTEN PEARS FOR ROTTEN PEERS

(22 October) There took place at Holyrood the election of 16 new Scottish peers to sit in the House of Lords. Perhaps not unsurprisingly, all were loyal to the new Hanoverian dynasty, 'a plain evidence of our further slavery to the English court', according to one contemporary. Another commentator, a woman selling fruit in the yard of the Palace, gave forth the following cries: 'Who would buy good pears, old pears, new pears, fresh pears – rotten pears, sixteen of them for a plack!'

1716

MINISTERS CAUGHT BETWEEN THE DEVIL AND THE DEEP-BLUE SEA

Two ministers, the Revd William Hamilton and the Revd William Mitchell, caused the presbytery of Edinburgh 'much grief and concern'. Their fault was to have broken the Sabbath by travelling through England on a Sunday. Called to explain themselves, the reverend gentlemen described how they had arrived at Stilton late on a Saturday evening, and found out that there was no Presbyterian church or dissenting meeting-house where they could worship the following day nearer than Stamford. They therefore decided to set off for Stamford on post-horses early on the Sunday morning, breaching one commandment in order to obey another. The explanation generally satisfied the presbytery, apart from a certain Revd James Webster, who roundly denounced his colleagues in the course of a prayer.

JACOBITES IN DRAG – PART II

(23 February) On the day before his execution for his part in the Jacobite Rising, William Maxwell, 5th Earl of Nithsdale, was visited in the Tower of London by his wife Winifred. The Countess was accompanied by her friend Mrs Mills, with whom she lodged. Mrs Mills 'was of a very tall and slender make', and was to play a crucial role in the Countess's plan. Mrs Mills was to enter with a handkerchief held to her face, 'as was very natural for a woman to do when she was going to bid her last farewell to a friend on the eve of his execution'. The Countess smuggled in a spare set of women's clothes identical to those worn by Mrs Mills, and after some French-farce-style to-ings and fro-ings she so managed things that she found herself alone with her husband. He immediately donned the female apparel his wife had brought, while she in turn saw to his cosmetic transformation. His dark eyebrows were painted the same sandy colour as those of Mrs Mills, his face whitened and his cheeks rouged. To top it all he put on 'an artificial head-dress of the same coloured hair' as that of Mrs Mills. And so, holding a handkerchief to his eyes as if in tears, he made good his escape from the Tower. Once reunited, the couple left for the Continent, and spent the rest of their days in contented penury in Rome.

1717

REVEREND GENTLEMAN RETURNS FROM OTHER WORLD

A contemporary leaflet recounted 'how Mr John Gardner, minister near Elgin, fell into a trance, and lay as dead for two days, in the sight of many; and how, being put into a coffin, and carried to his parish church in order to be buried, he was heard at the last moment to make a noise in the coffin; which being opened, he was found alive, to the astonishment of all present'. The reverend gentleman subsequently 'related many strange things which he had seen in the other world'.

TUTOR SLAUGHTERS YOUNG CHARGES IN FIT OF PIQUE

Mr Gordon of Ellon, a wealthy Edinburgh merchant, had employed a young 'licentiate of the church' called Robert Irvine to be private tutor to his two young boys. Irvine was not altogether of sound mind, a contemporary account explaining that 'A gloomy view of predestination had taken hold of Irvine's mind, which, perhaps, had some native infirmity, ready to be acted upon by external circumstances to dismal results.' But Irvine was not all doom and gloom, and indeed took a shine to a serving-girl in the Ellon household. One day, the account explains, he was 'tempted to take some liberties with her'. This was observed by his two young charges, who reported the matter to their father, who in turn rebuked Irvine. The latter apologised, and was forgiven. But Irvine nursed his grievance, which gnawed deeper and deeper into his heart, leading him to conclude that there was only one course that would relieve him of his burden.

Irvine seized his opportunity on 28 April, when his master and mistress were away from home and he was left in charge of the two boys. Irvine took them for a walk in the country where St Andrew's Square now stands, letting them wander about collecting flowers and chasing butterflies, while he himself sat sharpening a knife. The account continues:

> Calling the two boys to him, he upbraided them with their informing upon him, and told them that they must suffer for it. They ran off but he easily overtook and seized them. Then keeping one down upon the grass with his knee, he cut the other's throat; after which he despatched in like manner the remaining one.

Irvine showed no discretion in committing his hideous crime in the open, and the alarm was raised by passers-by. Having failed to cut his own throat, he fled towards the Water of Leith, with the apparent intention of drowning himself. But he was quickly apprehended, taken to jail, and there 'chained down to the floor, as if he had been a wild beast'.

Irvine was brought to trial on 30 April, and sentenced to die. That evening a number of ministers attempted to bring Irvine to a realisation of his crime, an aim that was eventually achieved when the blood-stained clothes of the slaughtered boys were brought before him. This gruesome sight prompted Irvine to beg forgiveness of the boys' parents, 'and this they very kindly gave'. Irvine was hanged the following day, but not before his hands had been hacked off and pinned to the gibbet with the very weapon with which he had committed his crime. His body was then flung into a quarry-hole.

THE ALMIGHTY CELEBRATES THE OLD PRETENDER'S BIRTHDAY

(10 June) Edinburgh was struck by a thunderstorm of unusual ferocity. That day was the birthday of the Old Pretender, and at Canonmills two barbers of Jacobite sympathies were toasting their monarch and lamenting the fact that his birthday was marked neither by church bells nor by an artillery salute from the Castle. At that very moment a great thunderclap burst over the tavern where they were drinking, prompting one to remark, 'The people on earth will not adore their king; but you hear the Almighty is complimenting him with a volley from heaven.' His delight was short-lived, however, as the very next moment he and a woman next to him were struck by a bolt of lightning and immediately perished. A third person was badly burnt, and died a few hours later. A contemporary account relates the curious circumstance that the bodies of the victims were 'soft as wool'. Persons attempting to claim that the Almighty was thus clearly a supporter of the Hanoverians were disappointed to learn that the second Jacobite barber escaped unharmed.

1718

A PIN IN THE MINISTER'S EGG, AND OTHER OUTRAGES

The Revd MacGill of Kinross found his house troubled by poltergeists. First of all, the household cutlery disappeared, and then was discovered in the barn. Then all food brought to the table was found to contain pins. There was even a pin in the minister's egg. Then sheets and clothing, whether in cupboards, hanging to dry, or worn on the persons of the household, were unaccountably snipped to pieces. One day a stone came down the chimney, bounced across the floor and then flew out the window. Finally, a plate and two silver spoons, together with the family Bible, were hurled by unseen hands into the fire. The Bible would not burn, but the other items melted. Robert Wodrow tells this story in his unpublished *Analecta*, concluding:

> Is it not very sad that such a godly family, that employ their time no otherwise but by praying, reading, and serious meditation, should be so molested, while others who are wicked

livers, and in a manner avowedly serve the Wicked One, are never troubled?

SCRABSTER INFESTED WITH CATS

The house of a certain William Montgomery in Scrabster, Caithness, became infested with cats, as many as eight at a time gathering around his fire in the evening and making a hideous noise. Witnesses believed the cats were speaking among themselves. Montgomery and his servants took up arms against the invaders, striking one in the hindquarters with a dirk, and battering another couple to death. The bodies of the latter being thrown out, all were amazed to find the corpses gone in the morning. Suspicions of witchcraft were of course entertained, and when an old woman called Margaret Nin-Gilbert 'was seen by some of her neighbours to drop at her own door one of her legs from the middle', she was put under arrest by the sheriff. 'When old ladies begin to unhook their legs, and leave them in public places,' writes Robert Chambers in recounting this story, 'it is evident there must be something in it.' Margaret duly confessed that she and some of her cronies were wont to take the guise of cats, and that while she was in this form Montgomery had broken her leg, which had putrefied, obliging her to jettison it, as described by the witnesses. 'In the course of a short time,' writes Chambers, 'Nin-Gilbert died in prison, and this seems to have been an end to the affair.'

1719

A HYDROLOGICAL MYSTERY

(2 November) Overnight the River Don dried out, allowing children to gather up all the fish left floundering on the riverbed. It was only around noon the following day that the water began to return.

The phenomenon recurred some decades later, as described by the *Statistical Account*:

> About 1750, in a fine summer morning, between five and six o'clock, the bed of the River Don, for the space of three miles below the church of Dyce, was found entirely empty; and was passed and repassed by several persons who gathered fish that

lay sprawling in the bottom. No person observed the commencement of this uncommon phenomenon. About half an hour after its discovery, the water came down the channel again in a full body. This was occasioned probably by a chasm formed by some internal commotion of the earth, which was sensibly felt by some persons.

MEN IN PHYSICAL DANGER FROM NEW FEMALE FASHION

A censor of morals and mores called Robert Ker, an inhabitant of Lasswade in Midlothian, published a brief jeremiad entitled *A Short and True Description of the Great Incumbrances and Damages that City and Country is like to sustain by Women's Girded Tails, if it be not speedily prevented, together with a Dedication to those that wear them.* 'Girded tails' were the steel hoops used to frame skirts, a fashion that was at this time sweeping the country – and sweeping gentlemen off their feet, if Ker is to be believed. 'Bordered by metallic cooperage,' Ker ranted, 'men walk the streets under hazard of breaking their shin bones.' It was impossible to pass a lady in a doorway or on a stair – at least, not without the risk of being called 'impertinat'. To keep Scottish manhood safe from unwitting collisions with these 'monstrous protuberances', Ker calls for all dark entries to be supplied with lights, and for appropriate alter-ations to staircases, coaches and churches. Even the wives and daughters of the clergy sport the fashion, Ker laments, bemoaning the absence of a John Knox to admonish the fair sex to its collective face. Although there is a certain irony in Ker's satire, he was himself a proven misogynist, being imprisoned on two occasions for mistreating his wife.

1720

WHIPPING FAILS TO ROUSE BOY FROM TRANCE

In Calder, Midlothian, the Hon. Patrick Sandilands, third son of Lord Torphichen, began to exhibit certain strange symptoms. The boy passed water 'black as ink', and sometimes he would appear to be thrown about the room, while at other times would seem to be suffering dreadful torments. He would often fall into trances, from which not even a severe horse-whipping could rouse him. He claimed to be able to fly through the air, and so a close watch was kept on him. On one occasion, the watcher having been distracted, the boy managed to get to the open door 'and was lifted in the air, but was catched by the heels and coat-tails, and brought back'. An old woman of the locality was arrested on suspicion of having bewitched him, but her fate is unclear. As for the boy, he eventually recovered, and joined the East India service, rising to captain one of the company's ships, and later drowned in a storm.

THE FAIR SEX DO NOT LOVE TO BE SURPRISED

A certain Adam Petrie published in Edinburgh *Rules of Good Deport-ment and Good Breeding*. He advised that 'a gentleman ought not to run or walk too fast in the streets, lest he be suspected to be going a message [i.e. running an errand]'. Just as gentlemen ought never to be taken for servants, those of inferior rank should at every occasion acknowledge their lowly position: 'When you give or receive anything from a superior, be sure to pull off your glove, and make a show of kissing your hand, with a low bow after you have done.' When entering the house of a 'great person', a gentleman should take off his greatcoat and his boots, but keep on his gloves – although 'it is usual in many courts that they deliver up their gloves with their sword before they enter the court, because some have carried in poison on their gloves, and have conveyed the same to the sovereign that way'. The drinking of tea, coffee and chocolate he denounces as 'irreligious tippling', for 'not one in a hundred asks a blessing to it'. Needless to say, playing at cards or dice, theatre-going and 'promiscuous' dancing are all beyond the pale. As for dealings with 'the fair sex', he advises that one should not enter their company 'without giving them time to appear to advantage: they do not love to be surprised'.

1721

YOUNG GENTLEMAN DIES OVER FORGOTTEN INSULT

In a note in *The Lay of the Last Minstrel*, Sir Walter Scott recounts the custom of biting one's own thumb or glove as a 'pledge of mortal revenge', and tells of an incident that took place in 1721:

It is yet remembered that a young gentleman of Teviotdale, on the morning after a hard drinking bout, observed that he had bitten his glove. He instantly demanded of his companions with whom he had quarrelled? and learning that he had had words with one of the party, insisted on instant satisfaction, asserting that, though he remembered nothing of the dispute, yet he never would have bitten his glove without he had received some unpardonable insult. He fell in the duel . . .

1722

ARMY OFFICERS INDULGE IN MUTUAL SKEWERING

(8 August) Two army officers, Captain Chiesley and Lieutenant Moodie, encountered each other in Edinburgh's Canongate. The former, remembering an earlier slight to his feelings, enquired of the latter 'whether he had in a certain company called him a coward'. The lieutenant owning that he had, 'the captain beat him first with his fist, and then with a cane':

> whereupon Mr Moodie drew his sword, and, shortening it, run the captain into the great artery. The captain, having his sword drawn at the same time, pushed at Mr Moodie, who was rushing on him with his sword shortened, and thus run him into the lower belly, of which in a few minutes he died, without speaking one word, having had no more strength or life left him than to cross the street, and reach the foot of the stair of his lodgings, where he dropped down dead. The captain lived only to step into a house near by, and to pray shortly that God might have mercy on his soul, without speaking a word more. 'Tis said Mr Moodie's lady was looking over the window all the while this bloody tragedy was acting.

1724

TAPPING AND SCRAPING HEARD FROM INSIDE COFFIN

Margaret Dickson, an Edinburgh fishwife, was charged under the Concealment of Pregnancy Act, having failed to register the birth of her illegitimate child, which died shortly afterwards. Such concealment was then a capital offence, and Maggie was sentenced to be hanged in the Grassmarket. After she was cut down, her body was placed in a coffin and put on a cart to take her for burial in her home parish of Musselburgh. But during the course of the journey the driver heard a desperate tapping and scraping coming from inside the coffin. The lid was opened, and there was Dickson, still alive. Her survival was considered to be due to Divine Providence (although some said she had seduced the ropemaker to persuade him to weaken the noose), and she was allowed to continue her life a free woman, achieving celebrity status as 'Half-hangit Maggie'. She lived another 40 years.

A PLUMP BURD

(2 June) The wife of Captain Burd of Ford was buried in Greyfriars Kirkyard. She was thought to be the largest woman in Scotland, her coffin measuring more than four feet wide and two feet deep.

1725

PRISONER TOLD: HANG OR BE HANGED

The burgers of Banff advertised for a new hangman, but to no avail. Perhaps no one wanted the job because one of the duties of the town's hangman was to clear the streets of horse droppings and dog mess. Eventually the job was offered to Robert Young, who at the time was in jail awaiting his own execution. It was an offer he could not refuse; if he did, he was told, he would be hanged.

1726

WICKEDNESS IS COME TO A TERRIBLE HEIGHT

(May) Robert Wodrow, minister at Eastwood, reported that the secretary of the English Hell-fire Club had arrived in Edinburgh with the intention of establishing an affiliated club in Scotland. But his plans came to nought, Wodrow tells us:

> He fell into melancholy, as it was called, but probably horror of conscience and despair, and at length turned mad. Nobody was allowed to see him, and physicians prescribed bathing for him, and he died mad at the first bathing. The Lord pity us, wickedness is come to a terrible height!

If one is to believe Wodrow, there appears to have been something of a vogue for such 'sulphur societies' as the Hell-fire Club, devoted to profanity and debauchery (see under 1732 for a well-documented example). Many persons of rank were thought to be members and office-holders, with such titles as Elisha the Prophet, the King of Hell, Old Pluto, the Old Dragon, Lady Envy, the Lady Gomorrah, and so on. What was truth and what was rumour is difficult to tell, but well into the following century, Robert Chambers tells us, the country people would recall such and such a laird whose membership of one of these sulphur societies had resulted in a 'bad end'.

SEXAGENARIAN UPHOLDS NATIONAL PRIDE

(June) A professional fencer, a young Irishman called Andrew Bryan, arrived in Edinburgh from London, where he had acquired great fame in one of the popular amusements of the age – public combats with sword and rapier. For several days Bryan paraded the streets of the Scottish capital with a drum, issuing a general challenge to the populace, but without receiving a single response. At last a former soldier called Donald Bane – a veteran of Killiecrankie, and now aged 62 – met Bryan in the street and kicked his foot through the Irishman's drum, so indicating that he accepted the challenge. On 23 June the two met on a stage especially erected behind Holyrood Palace, 'in the presence of a great number of noblemen, gentlemen, military officers, and others'. The affair was conducted with much formality, and lasted several hours. The upshot was that, after many rounds using different weapons, the young Irish blade had sustained a total of seven wounds, while the sturdy old Scot remained without a scratch. Much verse was scribbled in celebration of the national victory, although this was in Latin rather than Scots.

POET PRAISED FOR BOOKBINDING SKILLS

The Border poet James Thomson published 'Winter', the first part of *The Seasons*, and proudly presented a finely bound volume to his uncle, a man more practical than poetic. On receiving the gift, the old man turned the book over and over and, never once looking inside, exclaimed, 'Come, is that really our Jamie's doin' now? Well, I never thought the cratur hae had the handicraft to dae the like!'

1727

DEAD MAN WILLS THAT HIS FRIENDS GET DRUNK

(20 March) Death of Lord Forglen, judge of the Court of Session. On the day of his demise his physician, Dr Clerk, was admitted to his house by the judge's clerk, David Reid. On entering, Dr Clerk asked 'How does my lord do?'

'I hoop he's weel,' said the clerk, clearly implying that the old judge had died, and had passed over to a better life.

He then conducted his visitor into a room where two dozen bottles of wine were laid out, and here he was shortly joined by a number of other visitors. Reid proceeded to pour out glasses of wine and hand them around. After the visitors had taken a glass or two they rose to go, but Reid would have none of it. 'No, no, gentlemen,' he said, with tears streaming down his cheeks. 'Not so. It was the express will o' the dead that I should fill ye a' fou, and I maun fulfil the will o' the dead.'

'And indeed,' Dr Clerk recalled, 'he did fulfil the will o' the dead, for before the end o't there was nane o' us able to bite his ain thoomb.'

WOMAN BURNT FOR RIDING DAUGHTER

(June) A woman called Janet Horne was burnt to death in a tar barrel in Dornoch, Sutherland. She had been convicted of riding her daughter, having first turned her into a pony and having her shod by the Devil. As proof of the charge, it was noted that the girl was for ever after lame in both hands and feet. Janet Horne was the last person in Scotland to be burnt for witchcraft. Tradition holds that 'after being brought out to execution, the weather proving very severe, she sat composedly warming herself by the fire prepared to consume her, while the other instruments of death were making ready'.

1728

ROBBERS FORCED TO MUTILATE ONE ANOTHER

(10 December) Travelling over Soutra Hill in the Lammermuirs, a gentleman was held up by two men armed with bayonets, who demanded his purse. Reaching inside his coat, the gentleman produced not his purse but a pistol. At this the would-be robbers begged for their lives, explaining that necessity had forced them into crime, and that they had only robbed one other person, just an hour before. The gentleman took it upon himself to play both judge and jury in the case, and gave the men at his mercy a choice: 'either receive his bullets, or cut an ear out of each other's head; the last of which with sorrowful hearts they performed'.

1729

YOUNG MAN VOMITS UP OWN LUNGS

(24 February) The *Edinburgh Courant* reported the case of a young man of Glencorse who 'hath been grievously tormented by wicked spirits, who haunted his bed almost every night. There was no formed disease upon him; yet he had extraordinary paroxysms, which could not proceed from natural causes. He vomited vast quantities of blood, which was like roasted livers, and at last, with violent cries, his lungs.'

1731
TIGHT-ROPE THRILLS FROM THE CASTLE
TO THE GRASSMARKET

Edinburgh was visited by two tight-rope performers, a father and son who had toured all over Europe. Fixing a rope between the Half-Moon Battery on the Castle and the southern side of the Grassmarket some 200 feet below, the father slid down the rope in half a minute, followed by his son, who blew a trumpet throughout his journey, to the astonishment of 'an infinite crowd of spectators'. They repeated the feat three days later, and on this occasion the father climbed back up the rope to the Castle, beating a drum and firing a pistol and performing other tricks on the way. Exhausted by his efforts, he offered the sutler of the Castle a guinea for a draft of ale, 'which the fellow was churlish enough to refuse'.

A few weeks later an Edinburgh mason called William Hamilton attempted a similar feat across the defile of the Water of Leith at the Dean Village. He fell, and was killed.

1732
POSTURE MOLLS REVEAL THE SECRETS OF NATURE

In Anstruther, Fife, a minor Highland chieftain and customs official called John McNachtane of Dundarave founded The Most Ancient and Most Puissant Order of the Beggar's Benison and Merryland. 'Merryland' was 18th-century slang for the female body, while the 'Beggar's Benison' alluded to a story told about James V, who had wandered his kingdom disguised as 'the Goodman of Ballengeich'. One day while travelling in the East Neuk of Fife the Goodman, passing himself off as a piper, came to a burn in spate, and was unable to proceed until a sturdy female beggar hoisted up her petticoats and lifted him across. The Goodman rewarded her with a coin, in response to which she gave the following 'benison' or blessing: 'May your purse ne'er be toom [empty] and your horn aye [always] in bloom.' This became the inspiration for the club's motto, 'May prick nor purse ne'er fail you', and of its symbol, a phallus with a small bag dangling beneath it.

Meetings of the Beggar's Benison involved much eating and drinking, singing of ribald songs and toasting of ribald toasts – the members would raise their glasses to 'Firm erection, fine insertion, excellent distillation, no contamination.' Sex seems to have been an obsession, and the club hosted instructional lectures in that field, sometimes illustrated by naked 'posture molls', local girls who would adopt acrobatic positions in order to reveal 'the Secrets of Nature'. The club also maintained an extensive library of pornography. The initiation ceremony appears to have involved bouts of collective masturbation, apparently as an expression of free thinking. The club initially drew its members from the ranks of customs officers, merchants and well-off artisans. Branches were later established in Edinburgh, Glasgow and St Petersburg, and membership was extended to churchmen and aristocrats such as the Earl of Elgin, the Earl of Lauderdale and the Duke of Gordon. George IV became an honorary member when Prince of Wales, and donated a snuffbox containing the pubic hair of one of his mistresses. It is said that the club's many relics (including phallus-shaped drinking vessels and platters depicting erections in the form of lighthouses) were once offered to a museum curator, who, shocked by their explicit nature, fell into a faint.

DEAD DOGS THROWN INTO GRAVE OF NOTED RAKE

Death of the noted rake Colonel Francis Charteris at his estate near Musselburgh. He was buried in Greyfriars Kirkyard in Edinburgh, but such was his reputation for foul deeds, wrote Alexander Pope, that 'The populace at his funeral rais'd a great riot, almost tore the body out of the coffin, and cast dead dogs, &c., into the grave along with it.'

Born in (or near) Edinburgh, Charteris was the son of a respectable magistrate of that city. After a 'liberal education', he embarked on an inglorious career in the army, acquiring a reputation as a card-sharp; it was said that it was via a game of cards that he came by his colonel's commission. In 1711 Charteris was accused before the House of Commons of maintaining false muster records, recruiting debtors in return for a remuneration, and was obliged to fall to his knees while reprimanded by the Speaker. Despite this setback, he was appointed Deputy Lieutenant of Lancaster during the 1715 Jacobite Rebellion, trimming his sails from time to time according to which side appeared at that moment to be best favoured by fortune.

Pope provides a brief resumé of the Colonel's later career:

> After a hundred tricks at the gaming tables, he took to lending of money at exorbitant interest and on great penalties, accumulating premium, interest, and capital into a new capital, and seizing to a minute when the payments became due; in a word, by a constant attention to the vices, wants, and follies of mankind, he acquired an immense fortune. His house was a perpetual bawdy-house.

Having an apparently insatiable appetite for the charms of young women of the lower orders, Charteris employed 'Trusty Jack' Gourley to lure girls fresh from the country to his house in the West End of London, where, if they proved unwilling to submit to him, he would, it was said, force the issue. Charteris had been convicted of a rape at Musselburgh in 1722, but received a royal pardon; he was again accused in 1728, but seems to have got away with it once more.

In 1730 Charteris found himself summoned to the Old Bailey to face the accusations of his servant Anne Bond. Aware that his reputation might put off prospective female servants, he had assumed the name 'Colonel Harvey' in order to hire Bond, but once he started to make advances she realised who he was and asked to leave. Charteris had his staff prevent her from escaping, and the next morning he forced himself upon her. In court, his other servants swore that they had not seen or heard anything. When Bond told Charteris that she was going to report the assault, he informed his other servants that she had stolen money from him, and had them strip and whip her, then throw her out onto the street. The Old Bailey jury found Charteris guilty of rape, and he was held in Newgate Prison prior to the execution of his sentence of death. Charteris then used his ill-gotten fortune to mount a campaign for his release. Even Anne Bond (bribed, it was said, with the promise of an annuity) joined in, and in 1730 King George II granted him a pardon.

Posterity was not so kind. Hogarth based his *Rake's Progress* on Charteris, while Pope's friend John Arbuthnot penned the following epitaph:

HERE continueth to rot
The Body of FRANCIS *CHARTRES*,
Who with an inflexible constancy,
and Inimitable Uniformity of Life, Persisted,
In spite of Age and Infirmities,
In the Practice of Every Human Vice . . .

SOME SPRIGHTLY DAMES

(April) At the age of 80, Jean Johnston of Deer in Buchan married for the fourth time. Her new husband, an apprentice wheelwright, was aged only 18. She attributed her longevity to her 'many changes of husbands', and expressed the wish, should the current one not live long, that she should marry for a fifth time.

That same month, it was reported from Kirkcaldy that Margaret White, at the age of 87, had just cut eight fresh teeth. It was said that her husband was optimistic that 'she may bring him also a new progeny, as she has recovered, with her new tusks, a blooming and juvenile air'.

THE PRISONER OF ST KILDA

When Lady Grange, the estranged wife of James Erskine, Lord Grange, threatened to disclose her husband's role in the 1715 Jacobite Rebellion, he had her kidnapped from her lodgings in Edinburgh. With the aid of Lord Lovat and Macleod of Dunvegan, she was transported to the remote Monach Islands, to the west of North Uist, where she was kept prisoner for two years. Fearing that she might be discovered even in this remote spot, Lord Grange then had her moved to St Kilda, many more miles out into the Atlantic. Meanwhile, he announced her death, and put on a 'funeral' in Edinburgh with an empty coffin. Lady Grange remained on St Kilda until 1742, but managed to get a message to her brother, the Lord Advocate. But before the rescue party arrived, she had been moved again, to Assynt and then to Skye, where she was kept in a cave. She died there in 1745.

1736

AN EVENTFUL WEEK

(21 January) The *Caledonian Mercury* carried the following report from Lanark:

> A very uncommon chain of events happened here t'other week. Elizabeth Fairy was proclaimed in order to marriage on Sunday, was accordingly married on Monday, bore a child on Tuesday, her husband went and stole a horse on Wednesday, for which he was banished on Thursday; the heir of this marriage died on Friday, and was decently interred on Saturday – all in one week.

1738

THE OLD WOMAN WHO'D SEEN IT ALL

The following epitaph was composed for Margaret Scott of Dalkeith, who died at the supposed age of 125 years:

> Stop, passenger, until my life you read:
> The living may get knowledge of the dead.
> Five times five years I lived a virgin's life:
> Ten times five years I was a virtuous wife:
> Ten times five years I lived a widow chaste;
> Now, weary'd of this mortal life, I rest.
> Between my cradle and my grave have been
> Eight mighty kings of Scotland and a queen.
> Four times five years the Commonwealth I saw;
> Ten times the subjects rose against the law.
> Twice did I see old Prelacy pull'd down;
> And twice the cloak was humbled by the gown.
> An end of Stuart's race I saw: nay, more!
> My native country sold for English ore.
> Such desolations in my life have been,
> I have an end of all perfection seen.

1739
THE FIELDS SPREAD THICK WITH FISH

(14 January) So fierce was the wind storm that hit southern Scotland that 'At Loch Leven, in Fife, great shoals of perches and pikes were driven a great way into the fields; so that the country people got horse-loads of them, and sold them at one penny per hundred.'

1742
THE WAGES OF PIETY

(10 October) The northern Highlands were hit by an unusually early and heavy fall of snow. At Fearns in Ross-shire, it being a Sunday, the people were gathered to worship in the old church, when suddenly the weight of snow on the flagstone roof proved too much for the ancient structure and it collapsed upon the congregation below. The gentry, sheltering in their allocated side recesses, escaped largely unharmed, but many of the poor people were less fortunate. Forty of them 'were dug out dead, and in such a state of mutilation that it was found necessary to huddle them all into one grave'.

1743
LAST WOLF IN SCOTLAND SLAIN

The last wolf in Scotland was killed by a man called MacQueen in the upper reaches of the River Findhorn, by the Monadhliath mountains. The circumstances of this extinction are described by Charles Henry Alston in his *Wild Life in the West Highlands* (1912):

> The story is that a message was brought to MacQueen, a man of gigantic stature and noted for his courage and prowess as a hunter, that a 'large black beast' had killed two children, and requiring him to join his chief, the MacIntosh of that day, with his dogs for a great hunt on the following day. In the morning all were at the gathering place, except MacQueen, whose non-appearance greatly irritated the Chief; and when at last MacQueen made his appearance he was received with

impatience and remonstrance. 'What is the hurry?' said MacQueen, unfolding his plaid and throwing down the newly severed head of the wolf at the MacIntosh's feet. 'There it is for you'; and the tradition further tells how he was rewarded by his Chief with the grant of the lands of Seann-achan ...

1744
TEA FIT ONLY FOR THE WEAK, INDOLENT AND USELESS

Although the drinking of tea was becoming more popular in Scotland, many considered the beverage, in comparison to beer, to be 'an improper diet, expensive, wasteful of time, and calculated to render the population weakly and effeminate'. In Ayrshire a group of farmers signed a bond stating:

> We, being all farmers by profession, think it needless to restrain ourselves formally from indulging in that foreign and consumptive luxury called tea; for when we consider the slender constitutions of many of higher rank, amongst whom it is used, we conclude that it would be but an improper diet to qualify us for the more robust and manly parts of our business; and therefore we shall only give our testimony against it, and leave the enjoyment of it altogether to those who can afford to be weak, indolent, and useless.

1745
TAKING THE SIDE OF THE GALLOWS

At the commencement of the Jacobite Rebellion, a man was asked by his friend which side he intended to support. 'Faith,' the man replied. 'I shall take the side that the gallows is to be on.'

PRETENDING TO BE THE PRETENDER

(June) One David Gillies of Fife assumed the identity of Prince Charles Edward Stuart, the Young Pretender, and in this guise succeeded in obtaining money from many gullible Jacobite sympathisers. Eventually justice caught up with Gillies in Selkirk, where he and his 'court', consisting of two men and two women, were sentenced to be drummed out of the county.

A CLERK'S COURAGE

(September) Among the Edinburgh Volunteers preparing to join the regular forces of Sir John Cope, shortly to be routed by the Jacobites at Prestonpans, was a man described as follows by Sir Walter Scott:

> We remember an instance of a stout Whig and a very worthy man, a writing-master by occupation, who had esconced his bosom beneath a professional cuirass, consisting of two quires of long foolscap writing-paper; and, doubtful that even this defence might be unable to protect his valiant heart from the claymores, amongst which his impulses might carry him, had written on the outside, in his best flourish 'This is the body of J—— M——, pray give it Christian burial.'

1746

THE FORTUNES OF WAR

(17 January) At the Battle of Falkirk Muir, a certain Major Macdonald succeeding in dismounting a Hanoverian dragoon officer. Macdonald then mounted the horse, but could not then prevent it from taking its wonted place at the head of the Hanoverian cavalry. Unfortunately for Macdonald, the cavalry was in headlong retreat, and so Macdonald was captured and later executed for treason.

Another curious circumstance attending this, the last Jacobite victory of the '45 Rising, was the fact that General John Cope had laid bets totalling 10,000 guineas around the coffee houses of London that the next general sent north to Scotland would be beaten, as Cope himself had been defeated at Prestonpans the previous year. This fate overtook General Henry Hawley at Falkirk Muir.

A DARK SENSE OF HUMOUR

(March) Blair Castle was held for the government against a superior Jacobite force by Sir Andrew Agnew of Lochnaw, despite the fact that he and his men faced starvation. When the garrison was eventually relieved by the Earl of Crawford, Sir Andrew greeted him thus: 'My lord, I am very glad to see you; but, by all that's good, you have been very dilatory; we can give you nothing to eat.'

Sir Andrew, who had begun his distinguished military career under Marlborough, earned a reputation for personal courage combined with a teasing way with the men under his command. After one battle, he was approached by an orderly, who enquired of him: 'Sir, there is a heap of fellows lying yonder, who say they are only wounded, and won't consent to be buried like the rest. What shall I do?'

'Bury them at once,' insisted Sir Andrew, 'for if you take their own word for it, they won't be dead for a hundred years to come.' The orderly, though perplexed, nevertheless departed as if to carry out his orders, requiring Sir Andrew to issue a rapid countermand.

On another occasion, Sir Andrew had been much plagued by an importunate visitor to his house, who was so thick-skinned that he failed to notice how unwelcome he was. 'In troth,' said Sir Andrew, relaying this story to a friend, 'I was obliged to give the chiel a *broad hint*.'

'A broad hint?' replied the friend. 'I thought he was one of those who could not take a hint.'

'By my faith,' said Sir Andrew, 'but he was *forced* to take it. For, as the fellow would not gang out by the *door*, I threw him out of the *window*.'

THROWING UP A WARDROBE

There is a story of two Jacobite brothers who were captured by the Redcoats and held captive in a granary in Preston. Prior to his capture, one of the brothers had been shot, and the musket ball had taken a fragment of his scarlet waistcoat deep into his body. Jacobite prisoners were dealt with harshly, and those held in the Preston granary were no exception, being stripped by their captors down to their shirts. The wounded man became more and more sick, and in due course vomited up the patch of scarlet waistcoat that had penetrated his stomach. 'Oh, man, Watty!' exclaimed his brother. 'If you have got a wardrobe in your wame [belly], I wish you would throw me up a pair of breeks, for I have meikle need of them.' The wound eventually healed.

BAGPIPES JUDGED AN INSTRUMENT OF WAR

James Reid was one of a number of pipers who played the Highland clans into battle at Culloden. After the defeat of the Jacobites, he was captured, taken to York, and put on trial for treason. He argued that he had carried neither gun nor sword at the battle, only the pipes. However, the judges deemed the bagpipes to be 'an instrument of war', and sentenced the unfortunate Reid to be hanged, drawn and quartered.

NOBLES DEBATE PRECEDENCE ON SCAFFOLD

Two noble Jacobites, the Earl of Kilmarnock and Lord Balmerino, were condemned to be beheaded on Tower Hill. The normal rules of precedence would have demanded that Kilmarnock, the superior peer, take his turn first, but he graciously suggested to Balmerino that he might precede him. The sheriffs, however, were sticklers for correct procedure, and Kilmarnock accordingly was the first to lose his head.

JACOBITES IN DRAG – PART III

Bonnie Prince Charlie famously escaped 'over the sea to Skye' disguised as 'Betty Burke', Flora MacDonald's maid. The Prince was eager to conceal a pistol in his petticoat, but Flora objected, saying that if it were found they would be betrayed. The Prince said that if he were to be searched that closely, 'they would certainly discover me at any rate'. Not surprisingly, the appearance of the tall, wide-stepping 'maid' caused some alarm. When he appeared at the house of MacDonald of Kingsburgh, where he was to stay, his host's wife described 'Miss Burke' as an 'odd muckle trallup of a carlin [old woman]', and was further affrighted when the Prince, who had not shaven for some days, gave her a kiss.

VILLAINS, YOU HAVE KILLED YOUR PRINCE!

Finding himself once more on the mainland, the fugitive Prince was kept hidden from the pursuing Redcoats by the Seven Men of Glen Moriston, former soldiers in the Jacobite army who had taken refuge in the wilds. As it happened, a young merchant called Roderick Mackenzie, who bore a 'remarkable resemblance' to the Prince, was at that time travelling through Glen Moriston. A party of Redcoats spotted him, and, believing that the £30,000 reward offered by the government was almost theirs, they set off in pursuit. Mackenzie was overtaken, and shot. Loyal to the Jacobite cause, Mackenzie maintained the deception to the end, crying, 'Villains, you have killed your Prince!' The Redcoats took Mackenzie's head to Fort Augustus in triumph, and it was only then that their mistake was realised. In the meantime, the Prince was heading for the west coast, and the safety of a French frigate.

ESPRIT DE L'ESCALIER

Held in Edinburgh on suspicion of Jacobite sympathies, the brother-in-law of Lord Lovat (beheaded for treason the following year) was being interrogated by Hanoverian officers. He was indignant when one suggested that he had wished well to the rebels while they occupied Edinburgh.

'*Me?*' he exclaimed. '*Me* wish them weel? A pack o' nasty, lousy, low-lived scoundrels – as I tell'd them they were – that would never do ony gude in this world, but gang to the next on a widdy [hangman's rope].'

The officers were astonished. 'Did you really tell them so?'

'That I did indeed,' the prisoner replied, then added in a whisper, 'Only I loot them be twa mile awa' first.'

1747

TICKLISH ISSUES CONCERNING THE LOYAL TOAST

Around this time an English regiment was stationed in Peterhead. The Colonel of the regiment, wishing to be on good terms with the locals, invited Bishop Dunbar to dine with him. The old clergyman, a man of Jacobite sympathies, declined the invitation, citing his age and infirmities. The Colonel was persistent, but the Bishop continued to demur, saying that 'his principles forbade him to join in certain public toasts'. The Colonel promised 'that no toast should be given at all calculated to offend the feeling of the guest'. So in the end the Bishop found himself obliged to accept the invitation. All went well at the dinner, until a toast was given to 'The King'. The Bishop joined in the toast, but not without inserting the word 'rightful'. A young cornet was outraged, exclaiming, 'That is not King George, sir!' The Bishop was delighted. 'I take you all to witness,' he said, a twinkle in his eye, 'this young gentleman says King George is not our rightful sovereign!' Fortunately for the Bishop, the company saw the lighter side of the situation.

1749

SWEET MAY WEDS CROOKED JANUARY

(23 October) At the Canongate in Edinburgh, a Bluegown (licensed beggar) by the name of Hamilton, aged about 80, married Jean Lindsay, aged about 20, the daughter of another Bluegown. The disparity of age was remarkable enough. But, as the *Scots Magazine* observed, the physical attributes of the old man were even more remark-able:

> This man is one of the most deformed creatures, perhaps, in the whole world, and is well known all over Britain, having for a long time been carried about on an ass as an object of charity. He is so bowed together that his breast lies between his ankles; his knees on each side are higher than his back; and almost every member of his body is distorted.

1755

MINISTER SUFFERS AN INCURABLE *FUROR SCRIBENDI*

To universal derision, the Revd Walter Anderson published his *History of Croesus, King of Lydia*. Anderson was described by a later biographer as 'a respectable clergyman of mediocre talents, who was afflicted with an incurable *furor scribendi* [writing fury]'.

Anderson was minister at Chirnside in Berwickshire, and embarked on his lacklustre literary career following an encounter with the philosopher and historian David Hume, in which the subject of the latter's success as an author arose. 'Mr David,' Anderson remarked, 'I daresay other people might write books too; but you clever folks have taken up all the good subjects. When I look about me, I cannot find one unoccupied.' Amused at the bumptiousness of his interlocutor, Hume decided to wind the man up by suggesting that a history of

Croesus, king of Lydia, had yet to be written. Anderson took the great man at his word and, after considerable labour, in 1755 published his *History of Croesus*. The work was mockingly received in the *Edinburgh Review*, in an anonymous notice that in all likelihood was penned by Hume himself:

> Croesus king of Lydia is a prince whom we never expected to have met with, as the hero of a serious history . . . how unfortunate and ill-timed is our author's attempt to recall from oblivion the name and adventures of a monarch of such distant and dubious fame.

The reviewer goes on to regret Anderson's obsession with 'oracles, dreams, prodigies, miraculous interpositions of gods, and no less miraculous instances of credulity and folly among men', and continues:

> We conclude with an admonition to the author. In any future performance, we advise him either to venture into the region of pure fiction, or to confine himself within the precincts of real history . . .

Anderson's work was equally well received in the new *Critical Review*, edited by Tobias Smollett. The reviewer (probably Smollett himself) complained that the book exhibited a miserable flatness of style, and that all the facts scattered through its 255 pages might have been related in four. 'The subject,' he continues, 'is too meagre to afford nourishment to the fancy or understanding; and one might as well attempt to build a first-rate man of war from the wreck of a fishing-boat . . .'

Undeterred, Anderson churned out a succession of hugely tedious volumes on the history of France, apparently selling off some properties he owned in Duns to subsidise his folly. In 1789 Anderson published a pamphlet regretting the French Revolution, and when this too failed to sell, produced an appendix, ten times as long, justifying the arguments outlined in the shorter work. In his *Biographical Dictionary of Eminent Scotsmen* (1835), Robert Chambers summed up the man thus:

He is a remarkable specimen of that class of authors who, without the least power of entertaining or instructing their fellow-creatures, yet persist in writing and publishing books, which nobody ever reads, and still, like the man crazed by the lottery, expect that the next, and the next, and the next will be attended with success.

SHETLANDERS CHANGE COLOUR

Following a massive eruption in Iceland, Shetland was covered in a pall of volcanic ash, and anyone venturing outside ended up with a blackened face.

1760

A TRIPLE TRAGEDY

One day in April, two young lads were playing together at Stratton Mill near Edinburgh. It seems that the older boy told the younger that he would show him the way their father, a butcher, killed sheep, and with that he took up a knife and thrust it into the throat of his younger brother. Their mother, who was rocking an infant in its cradle, heard a scream and rushed to see what was the matter. The older boy, realising what he had done, fled, fell into the mill race and was swept down to the mill wheel, where he was crushed to death. The mother, realising there was no help for her dead boys, returned to the cradle to find that it had overturned, and her infant had been smothered in the bedclothes.

THE BOG THAT CURED SCROFULA

An old woman in Deeside suffering from scrofula had a vision in a dream that she would be cured if she plunged into a bog at the foot of Pannanich Hill. Putting the dream into practice, she found the bog did indeed prove an effective remedy. Hearing of this, Francis Farquharson of Monaltrie built a spa on the spot, which eventually grew into the town of Ballater.

THE FLOATING ISLAND OF LOCH LOMOND
AND OTHER TALL TALES

Publication of the anonymous *History of the Whole Realm of Scotland*, which has many curious things to say about the geography of the country, for example:

> By Inverness, the loch called Lochness, and the river flowing thence into the sea, doth never freeze: but on the contrary, on the coldest days of winter, the loch and river do smoke and reik, signifying to us, that there is a mine of brimstone under it, of a hot quality.

Loch Lomond, the author claims, is home to 'fishes, very delectable to eat, that have no fins to move themselves, as other fishes do'. Furthermore, even on the most windless of days, the loch is troubled by 'tempestuous waves and surges of the water, perpetually raging'. Finally, one of the islands of the loch, though possessed of good pasture which is fed on by cattle, 'moves by the waves of the water, and is transported, sometimes towards one point, and other whiles towards another'.

Another aquatic curiosity is described thus:

> In the north seas of Scotland, are great clogs of timber found, in the which are marvellously engendered a sort of geese, called Clayk Geese, and do hang by the beak, till they be of perfection . . .

This last claim is presumably based on the old belief that barnacle geese, who visit Europe every winter, were generated from tiny shells growing on trees. They were thus regarded as fish, and could therefore be eaten on fast days. However, as far back as 1597 sailors from William Barents's expedition to Novaya Zemlya in the Arctic Ocean had found the nests of barnacle geese, showing that they originate in the same way as other birds.

1761

THE LAST OF THE FEUDAL LORDS

(21 July) Death of Alexander Douglas, 1st Duke of Douglas, known as 'the last of the feudal lords'. He himself confessed that 'he could neither read nor write without great difficulty'. His pride was matched only by his quickness to take offence, and in 1725 he killed John Kerr, the bastard son of his brother-in-law, who had been wooing his sister, Lady Jane Douglas. The Duke was obliged to go abroad for a while, but later returned to Scotland and never faced any charges; it seems he was considered insane, and he subsequently became something of a recluse.

In 1758 the ducal seat, Douglas Castle, burnt down, and Douglas commissioned John Adam to design a new castle, which was to be ten feet higher and ten feet wider than the Duke of Argyll's new castle at Inveraray. While work on the new castle was under way, Douglas lived in Holyroodhouse in Edinburgh, where he had apartments. One day during his stay in Edinburgh he visited a barber in the city, and on entering the premises he drew his sword, telling the barber he would cut off his head should the barber inflict even the slightest nick. The barber reassured the Duke that he was safe in his hands, and so it proved. After the shaving was completed to everyone's satisfaction, the Duke asked the barber how he had kept his hand so steady, given the threat hanging over him. The barber told him that he had feared nothing, as if he *had* nicked His Grace he would have had the advantage: before the Duke could have reached his sword, he would have slit His Grace's throat from ear to ear. The Duke was highly amused, and left a generous tip.

In 1746, without his knowledge, Douglas's sister married Colonel John Stewart of Grandtully and fled to the Continent, only informing her brother of her marriage two years later, when she gave birth, at the age of 50, to twins. She was cut off without a penny, and it was only eight years after the Duke's death, and a lengthy lawsuit, that her son was allowed to inherit his estates.

1763

HIGHLAND INGENUITY

Towards the end of the French and Indian Wars, several members of Montgomerie's Highlanders (the 77th Regiment) found themselves captives of the Native Americans. There is a story that one of the prisoners, Allan Macpherson, was obliged to watch as his companions suffered slow and painful deaths. In order to avert such a fate for himself, he told his captors that if his life would be spared for a few minutes he would show them the secret of an extraordinary medicine, which, if applied to the skin, would provide protection against any weapon. His captors agreed that he could go into the woods with a guard to collect the necessary ingredients. Returning with handfuls of leaves, Macpherson brewed them up in a pot of water, then applied the resulting tincture to his neck. He then placed his head across a fallen tree trunk and invited the strongest brave to strike him with his tomahawk. The brave obliged, and with a mighty blow sent Macpherson's head shooting across the clearing. And so the soldier achieved a mercifully quick release, rather than a lingering death by a thousand torments.

1767

A FOUL-MOUTHED, SWEET-MOUTHED DUCHESS

Jane Maxwell, a noted society beauty dubbed 'the Flower of Gallo-way', married Alexander Gordon, 4th Duke of Gordon. Her manners caused one contemporary wag to observe:

> The Duchess triumphs in a manly mien;
> Loud is her accent, and her phrase obscene.

She took a number of lovers, so when Marquess Cornwallis, a suitor to one of her daughters, expressed concern about the streak of hered-itary madness in the Gordon line, she was able to reassure him that her daughter had not a drop of Gordon blood in her veins.

There is one story told about her (or possibly a later Duchess of Gordon), regarding the visit to Gordon Castle of an English noble-man. After some six weeks of shooting in the north, this young man claimed that he had acquired so much of the Scots tongue that it was impossible to baffle him. 'Then,' said the beautiful Duchess, 'come pree my mou, my canty callant.' The young man had to admit that he was foxed, and it was with some chagrin that he later realised what a chance he had lost: *pree* means 'try by tasting'.

A TWO-HEADED CHILD

In Galloway, the wife of a soldier gave birth to a child 'having two heads, four hands, four legs, and one body'.

1770

WHAT IS THE NILE TO THE MIGHTY CLYDE?

(4 November) While travelling in Abyssinia disguised as a Syrian physician by the name of El Hakim Yagoube, the Scottish explorer James Bruce of Kinnaird found a swamp near Gish that he claimed was the source of the Nile. In the 'sublime of discovery' he raised a glass to George III, Catherine the Great of Russia, and an unknown woman called Maria. The discovery may have been sublime, but the sight was, Bruce opined, 'trifling', in comparison to 'that majestic scene in my own country, where Tweed, Clyde and Annan rise on one hill'. The swamp near Gish was in fact just one of many tributaries of the Blue Nile, while the source of the White Nile, the major branch, turned out to be somewhere else altogether. Ironically, having survived innumerable dangers on his travels, in 1794 Bruce died after falling down the stairs at his home in Kinnaird.

1771

A CURE FOR DEAFNESS

A man from Irvine was cured from the deafness from which he had suffered for 20 years when he was struck by lightning.

THE SOLWAY BOGALANCHE

(17 November) During the night a natural calamity befell the people who farmed the lands adjacent to Solway Moss. Days of heavy rain had turned this extensive wetland into fluid black sludge, and, the

firmer edges of the Moss having been removed by peat-cutters, there was nothing to hold back the tidal wave of liquid bog. This proceeded to overwhelm everything in its path, overturning some buildings and filling others up to the ceiling, forcing the inhabitants onto the roof to await rescue. More than 400 acres of farmland were thus destroyed. In one byre only one cow out of eight survived. She was found nearly three days later up to her neck in mud. 'When she was relieved,' one account relates, 'she did not refuse to eat, but would not touch water, nor would even look at it without manifest signs of horror.'

1772

THE ENORMOUS SINNERS OF IONA

Thomas Pennant visited Iona, where he was told that near to the bay where Columba landed there was 'a vast tract . . . covered with heaps of stones of unequal sizes':

> These, as is said, were the penances of monks who were to raise heaps of dimensions equal to their crimes; and to judge by some, it is no breach of charity to think there were among them enormous sinners.

POTATO WILKIE, THE SCOTTISH HOMER

(10 October) Death, at the age of 51 from a 'lingering disposition', of Dr William Wilkie, minister, poet, and Professor of Natural Philosophy at the University of St Andrews. His best known poetical production was *The Epigoniad*, the story of the Epigoni, the descendants of the Seven Against Thebes. This 'long ponderous epic' (as the *Dictionary of National Biography* describes it) begins as it means to continue:

> Ye pow'rs of fong! with whofe immortal fire
> Your bard inraptur'd fung Pelides' ire,
> To Greece fo fatal, when in evil hour
> He brav'd, in ftern debate, the fov'reign pow'r;
> By like example, teach me now to fhow
> From love, no lefs, what dire difafters flow.

The poem went down badly in London, and as a consequence was championed north of the border, where Henry Mackenzie wrote that he and his literary friends considered Wilkie 'superior in original genius to any man of his time'. Wilkie became known as 'the Scottish Homer'; he also earned another epithet, 'Potato Wilkie' or 'the Potato Minister', owing to his enthusiasm for agricultural improvement.

Wilkie was a man of considerable eccentricity. Here is one description, from Alexander Hislop:

> He suffered so much from ague, that, to keep up a perspiration, he used to lie in bed with no less than two dozen blankets upon him; and, to avoid all chance of the cold damp, he never slept in clean sheets . . . His walking dress usually consisted of several flannel jackets, waistcoats, and topcoat; and over all a greatcoat and gown, which gave him a very grotesque appearance . . . Added to these peculiarities, he indulged in tobacco to an immoderate extent.

Wilkie was also notably absent-minded, on one occasion mounting the pulpit to preach oblivious of the fact that his hat still sat firmly on his head. But the kindness of his disposition, his gentleness and good humour, ensured that at his death he was mourned by many friends.

1773
A LAIRD CALLED MUCK

Dr Johnson, visiting the island of Coll, noted that Maclean of Coll, the laird, was simply known as 'Coll'. So when he visited the island of Muck he expected that the laird would call himself 'Muck'. Far from it: the embarrassed laird, insisting that the first laird of Muck had been a monk from Iona, informed Johnson that his title was not 'Muck' but 'Monk'.

1775

CHIEF OF THE CHEROKEES AND DELIVERER
OF THE JEWS

Death of Sir Alexander Cuming, baronet, traveller and 'enthusiast of great but misapplied talents'. Cuming was born in Edinburgh, the son of Sir Alexander Cuming of Culter in Aberdeenshire. As a young man, Cuming (or Cumming, or Comyn) held commissions in both the British and the Russian armies, and was called to the Scottish bar in 1714, but retired in 1718 when the government offered him a pension. In 1729 his wife, Lady Cuming (née Amy Whitehall), experienced a visionary dream that prompted her husband to travel to America to meet the chiefs of the Cherokee nation among the remote mountains of South Carolina and Virginia. At this meeting, which took place at Nikwasi on 3 April 1730, Cuming not only received the scalps of his hosts' enemies, but was elected commander and chief ruler of the Cherokee. He returned to Britain with seven of the chiefs, and on 18 June presented himself and his companions to George II at Windsor, laying his own crown at the king's feet.

In 1748 Cuming proposed a plan to the prime minister, Henry Pelham, by which provincial banks were to be established throughout the American colonies, a scheme that he linked to the 'restoration' of the Jews, 'for which he supposed the time appointed to be arrived, and that he himself was alluded to in various passages of Scripture as their deliverer'. To this end, he proposed to raise £500,000, and to settle 300,000 Jewish families among the Cherokee Mountains. Pelham treated Cuming as 'a visionary enthusiast', and nothing more came of the plan.

Cuming then turned to alchemical experimentation, but was unsuccessful in transmuting base metals into gold. Having failed to recoup his fortunes in this fashion, he fell increasingly into debt, and in 1737 was incarcerated as a debtor in London's Fleet Prison; he had already been expelled from the Royal Society for failing to pay his subscription. In 1766 he became a pensioner in the Charterhouse, a London charitable institution, where he died. His son Alexander, an army officer, 'became deranged in his intellects' and died a pauper.

1776

PHILOSOPHER GOES THROUGH THE MOTIONS

(25 August) Death of the philosopher David Hume. He had nearly met his death many years before, when he fell into a bog below Edinburgh Castle, no doubt a receptacle for at least some of the city's sewage. Becoming stuck, and apparently sinking, Hume called for assistance from a woman who happened to be passing.

'Are ye no Hume the atheist?' she demanded.

'Well, no matter,' Hume replied. 'Christian charity commands you to do good to everyone.'

'Christian charity here, Christian charity there,' replied the woman, 'I'll dae naethin for ye till ye turn a Christian yersel. Ye maun repeat the Lord's Prayer and the Creed, or faith I'll let ye grafel [flounder about] there as I fand ye.'

And so the sceptical philosopher was obliged to go through the required motions, in order to save his life.

1777

SOUL MATES TILL DEATH DID THEM PART

A newspaper published the following letter from Lanark:

> Old William Douglas and his wife are lately dead; you know that he and his wife were born on the same day, within the same hour, by the same midwife; christened at the same time, and at the same church; that they were constant companions till nature inspired them with love and friendship; and at the age of nineteen were married, by the consent of their parents, at the church where they were christened. These are not the whole of the circumstances attending this extraordinary pair. They never knew a day's sickness until the day before their deaths; and on the day on which they died were aged exactly one hundred years. They died in one bed, and were buried in one grave, close to the font where they were both christened. Providence did not bless them with any children.

1778

PRIVATEER REPULSED BY THE POWER OF THE PETTICOAT

When the Kirkcudbrightshire-born American patriot and privateer John Paul Jones sailed into Lerwick during the American War of Independence, he was alarmed to see the town crammed with what he took to be red-coated British soldiers. He immediately turned tail and sailed away. The figures he had taken for Redcoats were in fact the girls of the town, dressed in their traditional red petticoats.

MINOR POET HOPES FOR INSPIRATION FROM TOOTH OF BARD

Death of the great Gaelic poet Rob Donn. He was buried in Balnakeil, Sutherland, and it was said that a minor poet, hoping to inherit some of Rob Donn's genius, dug up his body and extracted one of his molars, in the belief that this would give him inspiration. The culprit thereafter suffered from terrible toothache, which only stopped once the molar had been returned to its proper place.

1782

FEEDING THE IDLE AND WORTHLESS ON THE PICKLED CORPSES OF SLAUGHTERED DOGS

The publisher William Creech, who wrote in the newspapers under the pseudonym 'Theophrastus', responded to the grain shortages of 1782 with the following proposals, supposedly unanimously voted for by a 'meeting of respectable citizens':

> 1st, That the frugal economy with regard to provisions should be observed; and that, with this view, all dogs, unless those of great use and value, should be instantly put to death.
> 2dly, That the food of man should not be consumed by vile animals.

The meeting was also unanimously of the opinion . . .

That all beggars, thieves, wh——s, discarded footmen, idle vagabonds, blackguards, and ballad-singers, who infest this city, should be instantly put to death, as they consume a great deal of good provision, and are not only useless but noxious animals.

There was some debate, inconclusive, as to whether 'players, tumblers, rope-dancers, fire-eaters, etc.' should be added to the list. Regarding the brains of the dead, 'the Meeting thought they might be sold as great bargains to the students of physic, and the money properly applied to support people worth preserving alive'. As to 'gamblers, the idle and worthless of both sexes, a considerable proportion of hairdressers, perfumers, footmen, chairmen, etc.', they 'ought, in the present scarcity of corn, to be reckoned vile and useless animals, and not to be permitted to consume the food of man'. Instead, they were to be fed the pickled corpses of slaughtered dogs.

Creech went on to become Lord Provost of Edinburgh from 1811 to 1813. As far as is known, he did not implement the above policies while in office.

1784
THE MOST IMPUDENT PUPPET-SHOW OF IMPOSITION

In order to escape his many creditors in London, 'Dr' James Graham returned to his native Edinburgh, where he had studied medicine but had failed to take a degree. For a while Graham had had a great success in London with his Temple of Hymen, where he welcomed a wealthy clientele suffering from nervous disorders. At the Temple his patients might be invited to bathe in milk or mud, sit on a 'magnetic throne', receive ice-cold champagne douches or electrical stimulation, or be 'agitated in the delights of love' on the famous Celestial Bed. His speciality was restoring sexual vigour, a procedure that may have been aided by the presence of scantily attired young women posing as Hebe Vestina, goddess of health (one of his models was Emma Lyon, later Lady Hamilton). Visiting the Temple of Hymen as a spectator, Horace Walpole described it as 'the most impudent puppet-show of imposition I ever saw'.

Back in Edinburgh, Dr Graham found that his public promotions of sexual health got him into trouble with the authorities, so he embarked on a new therapeutic venture, more suited to the self-mortifying inclinations of his Calvinistic fellow countrymen. Based on a theory that disease was caused by excess heat, Graham announced a plan to build a Spartan Temple of Health on top of Arthur's Seat, where the poorly would be exposed to all the bitter chills of the Edinburgh climate. The city council declined to give the plan their seal of approval, and the summit of Arthur's Seat remained untarnished.

Later in life Graham became something of a religious enthusiast, styling himself 'the Servant of the Lord O.W.L.' (Oh, Wonderful Love), and preaching the benefits of vegetarianism. This resulted in him being judged a lunatic, and his consequent temporary confinement to his house in Edinburgh. One of his last medical claims was that he had survived for a fortnight in midwinter on nothing but cold water, keeping his naked body warm by surrounding himself with turfs and rubbing his skin with his own patent aethereal balsam. Eighteen months after this experiment, on 23 June 1794, he suddenly expired, and was buried in Greyfriars Kirkyard.

ELSPETH BUCHAN AND THE RAPTURE THAT WASN'T

A small band, numbering no more than a few dozen people, gathered together on a hill in Dumfriesshire in the expectation that they would, in an instant, be transported to heaven. These were the Buchanites, the followers of Elspeth Buchan, whom the Revd Hugh White of the Irvine Relief Fund had identified as the woman described in Revelation 12:1:

> And there appeared a great wonder in heaven, a woman clothed with the sun, and the moon under her feet, and upon her head a crown of twelve stars.

Mrs Buchan, who referred to herself as 'Friend Mother in the Lord', claimed the gift of prophesy and believed that when she breathed on her followers, 'with postures and gestures that are scandalously indecent' (according to Robert Burns), she was giving them the Holy Ghost.

In 1784, as a consequence of his heterodox beliefs, the Revd White was expelled by his local presbytery in Irvine. Along with Mrs Buchan and a few disciples, he followed what he believed to be the star that had guided the Wise Men to Bethlehem. This led them to New Cample in Dumfriesshire.

After 40 days of fasting, Mrs Buchan judged that the time of the rapture was imminent, and instructed her followers to build a number of platforms on a nearby hill, with her own platform being the highest of all. The Buchanites had shaved their heads apart from a topknot, by which means, they believed, the angels might more easily raise them to heaven. Unfortunately things did not go to plan. A strong wind arose, and the platforms were blown over, tumbling the Buchanites in the opposite direction to that which they had expected to travel.

After this disappointment, Mrs Buchan's following diminished, owing to a combination of disillusionment and the celibacy she insisted upon. When she died seven years later, the Revd White insisted she was merely in a trance, but even he had to acknowledge his error when her body began to rot. The last Buchanite, Andrew Innes, died in 1846, having left instructions that he should be buried on top of Mrs Buchan, so that he would be woken when, at the Last Day, she arose to glory.

ENCYCLOPÆDIST TAKES TO THE
SKIES OVER EDINBURGH

(27 August) Taking off from Comely Gardens in Edinburgh, James Tytler made the first manned flight in Britain aboard his 'Grand Edinburgh Fire Balloon'. Once the balloon was inflated Tytler stepped into the small wicker basket, wearing a cork jacket to cushion his body should he fall. Finding no means of taking the coal brazier aloft, his flight was of necessity short, but he did manage to rise to a height of more than 300 feet, landing safely at Restalrig, about half a mile away.

Unfortunately, Tytler's achievement was eclipsed by the much more heavily publicised flight made in London a fortnight later by the showy young Neapolitan balloonist and diplomat Vincent Lunardi, who subsequently displayed his aerial feats in several parts of Scotland. As a consequence, Tytler's achievement was largely forgotten, and Lunardi generally credited with making the first balloon flight in Britain. In an effort to seize back some glory, on 11 October 1784 Tytler tried one more flight, which ended ignominiously when his balloon crashed before a crowd of paying spectators.

This was one of many low points in the life of a man described by Burns as 'an obscure, tippling though extraordinary body'. A son of the manse from Brechin, Tytler had studied medicine at Edinburgh University, helping to fund his studies by working as ship's surgeon on a Greenland-bound whaler. Once qualified, he set up as an apothecary in Leith, but his poor business sense (not helped by a weakness for strong drink) obliged him in 1766 to flee to Newcastle to escape his creditors. The previous year he had married Elizabeth Rattray, the daughter of a wealthy lawyer, with whom he had five children. The family returned to Edinburgh in 1773, but two years later he was declared bankrupt and separated from his wife, who had been discomposed by his liaison with the sister of the local butcher. Mrs Tytler subsequently set herself up as a grocer in the Canongate. Tytler himself later moved in with another woman, Jean Aitkenhead, with whom he had two children.

Tytler sought to eke out his meagre earnings as an apothecary with various literary ventures, which proved (as is the way of these things) to yield even more meagre pickings. In 1777 he accepted the post of editor of the second edition of the *Encyclopædia Britannica*, even though he was paid at less than half the rate received by his predecessor. Lodging with a washerwoman in Duddingston, Tytler would work on an upturned wash tub, and in this fashion he expanded the *Encyclopædia* from three to ten volumes, penning hundreds of new articles himself. He also embarked on a *General History of All Nations, Ancient and Modern*, but only succeeded in completing one volume. It was during his extensive researches into all sorts of subjects that Tytler learnt of the ballooning success of the Montgolfier brothers in France, which inspired his own aeronautical efforts.

Success was not to be a hallmark of Tytler's own career, however. In 1785 he was again declared bankrupt, and two years later his estranged wife sued for divorce. In 1788 he was once more obliged to leave for England to shake off his creditors, and did not return to Edinburgh for another three years. It was perhaps his personal sense of injustice that led Tytler towards the radical politics that swept Scotland in the wake of the French Revolution. In 1792 he published a handbill in which he condemned the House of Commons as a 'vile junto of aristocrats', and called for sitting members to be replaced by MPs of 'good understanding and character'. In the atmosphere of paranoid reaction then prevalent among the ruling classes, Tytler was charged with seditious libel, but before he could be tried he left Edinburgh for Belfast, and from thence, in 1795, he emigrated to Salem, Massachusetts, where his continuing lack of success as a hack writer plunged him deeper into despondency and alcohol dependency. It was while stumbling home from a drinking session on 9 January 1804 that he fell into the sea and drowned.

1786

LAWYER MISTAKEN FOR SCOUNDREL

Death of the irascible Edinburgh lawyer, Hugo Arnot, who was so thin that one of his contemporaries compared him to a dried haddock. In his professional role as an advocate Arnot could be touchy. Once, when approached by a potential client whose case he regarded as highly suspect, he enquired of the man, 'Pray, sir, what do you suppose me to be?'

'Why,' answered the man, 'I understood you to be a lawyer.'

'I thought,' Arnot drily retorted, 'you took me for a scoundrel.'

On another occasion he encountered, returning from the Grassmarket, his acquaintance George Hill, then tutor to the family of the Lord Justice Clerk and a candidate for the Chair of Humanity (i.e. Latin) at Edinburgh University. Arnot asked Hill what he had been doing in the Grassmarket. The latter replied that he had 'been seeing the execution' of three men.

'What!' exclaimed Arnot, 'You! George Hill, candidate for the professor's chair of Humanity?'

'Yes, Mr Arnot,' replied Hill sheepishly.

'Then, by God, you should rather be professor of barbarity. And you are sure of the situation, for it is in the gift of the Lord Justice Clerk.'

In the building where he lived, Arnot elicited frequent complaints from his upstairs neighbour, an old spinster, regarding the violence with which he would ring his bell to summon his servant. Eventually, worn down by her constant messages, he gave her to understand that he would desist from the practice. However, believing that her complaints arose from 'mere querulousness', whenever he wished to let his servant know that his presence was required he would discharge a loaded pistol – to the considerable alarm of the invalid upstairs, who as a consequence implored him to resume the use of the bell.

Having a presentiment of his own imminent death, Arnot would frequently visit the plot in South Leith kirkyard where he was to be buried, to urge the masons to make haste lest he expire before his grave should be completed. Among Arnot's literary works was *An Essay on Nothing*.

UNITED IN DEATH ON THE LONELY SHIANT ISLES

Captain Allan Morrison of Stornoway was betrothed to Annie Campbell of Scalpay, but tragedy intervened when Morrison, known as Ailein Duinn ('brown-haired Allan') was drowned in a storm at sea. His body was washed up on the shores of the Shiant Isles, off the south-east coast of Lewis. Annie, overwhelmed with grief, died of a broken heart. When her body was being taken across to Harris, the boat was struck by a storm, and to save themselves the sailors threw her coffin into the sea. Her body too ended up on the shores of the Shiant Isles, close to where her lover's body had been found. The story inspired a well-known Gaelic lament:

> Brown-haired Allan, o hi, I would go with thee;
> Ho ri ri u ho, e o hug hoireann o,
> Brown-haired Allan, o hit, I would go with thee.

FAILED POET DEVISES NEW
SYSTEM OF SPELLING

When James Elphinstone, the son of an Episcopalian minister from Edinburgh, tried his hand at verse, his offerings were dismissed by the critics as 'nonsense and gibberish'. He turned instead to the study of orthography, publishing *Propriety Ascertained in her Picture*, in which he proposed a more rational mode of spelling for the English language. His preface begins thus:

EVVERY tung iz independant ov evvery oddher. Hooevver *ſ*eeks dhe anallogy (or nattural rule) ov anny tung, mu*ſ*t dherfore find it at home: nor wil dhe *ſ*eeker *ſ*eek in vain. Ingli*ſ*h diccion dhen haz no laws, but her own. Yet, in her picturage, and con*ſ*equently in much ov her livving practice; hav anny oddher laws, or anny lawle*ſ*nes, been prefferably regarded. No more can anny language adopt dhe *ſ*y tem ov anny oddher; dhan anny nacion, dhe hoal pollity ov anoddher nacion: for *ſ*uch adopter wer no more a di tinct nacion or language; wer but a mongrel, or an eccoe.

The lack of commercial success of this work, and the follow-up volumes *English Orthography Epitomized* and *Propriety's Pocket Dictionary*, ate up Elphinstone's fortunes, and he might have died a pauper had not his sister and brother-in-law left him an annuity.

1787
SCOTLAND RULED BY AN IDIOT KING

(27 August) Robert Burns, 'heated with drink' as he later admitted, inscribed the following lines with a diamond on a window of an inn in Stirling:

> Here Stuarts once in glory reigned,
> And laws for Scotland's weal ordained;
> But now unroof'd their palace stands,
> Their sceptre's sway'd by other hands;
> The injured Stuart line is gone,
> A race outlandish fills their throne —
> An idiot race, to honour lost;
> Who know them best despise them most!

This attack on the reigning Hanoverian dynasty, in the person of the half-mad George III, got the poet into a spot of bother. He was, he wrote in a letter, visited by a 'great person' and subjected to an interrogation 'like a child about my matters, and blamed and schooled for my inscription on a Stirling window'. Burns returned to Stirling about two months later to smash the offending pane of glass with his riding crop. But by this time the lines had been much copied and circulated.

1788

ON THE HEALTH-GIVING BENEFITS OF
ALCOHOL AND OPIUM

Death of John Brown, the son of a Berwickshire labourer who went on to study medicine at Edinburgh. There he developed a novel system of treatment, based on his own experience. He had suffered badly from gout, and had been advised to give up both meat and alcohol, but as this advice was contrary to his inclinations he had once more given in to his appetite for hearty drinking and hearty fare, and had found himself gout-free for a period of six years. From this he developed his idea that all diseases resulted either from an excess of excitement, or a lack of it. Apoplexy, he averred, was an example of the former, and 'common fever' of the latter. Diseases due to over-excitement were to be treated by debilitating medicines, while those requiring stimulation were to be cured by means of wine, brandy and opium (all of which most authorities, then and now, would deem to have a sedative action). One of his pupils later described how, before he began a lecture, Brown himself would

> take fifty drops of laudanum in a glass of whisky, repeating the dose four or five times during the lecture. Between the effects of these stimulants and his voluntary exertions, he soon waxed warm, and by degrees his imagination was exalted into a phrensy.

Initially Brown attracted many students, but he so alienated the Edinburgh medical establishment that he was obliged to pursue his fortunes in London, where he continued his extravagant lifestyle and ended up in a debtors' prison. He was released early in 1788, but died on 7 October that year, having taken a considerable quantity of laudanum before going to bed, and suffered a fatal stroke of apoplexy during the night.

1790

A BRUTISH MUSICIAN

Around this time the Royal High School in Edinburgh had a master by the name of Nicol who found such fault with his charges that he would sometimes have a dozen of them lined up at once for a serial thrashing. On such occasions he would ask a fellow teacher 'to come and hear his organ'. He would then march up and down the row, beating each boy in turn, so composing a pleasing cacophony (to his ear at least) of squawks and howls.

RAIN A CERTAINTY

The *Statistical Account*, writing about Lochcarron, was moved to bemoan the weather:

> The seasons are always wet in this place, but within these few years they seem to be turning worse. Everything almost is reckoned a sign of rain. If there be a warm or hot day, we shall soon have rain; if a crow begins to chatter, she is calling for rain; if the clouds be heavy, or if there be a mist on the top of the hills, we shall see rain. In a word, a Highlander may make anything a sign of rain: there is no danger he shall fail in his prognostication.

1792

CIVIC PRIDE

Provost Kerr of Peebles travelled to London as a delegate to discuss the issue of burgh reform. While there he attended a dinner at the Whig Club, where Charles James Fox proposed a toast 'To the Majesty of the People'. Kerr misheard this as 'To the Magistrates of Peebles', and, puffed up with his own importance, stood up and delivered a pompous speech of acknowledgement, 'to the no small amazement and diversion of the whole company'.

1793
A DUMB SPIRIT

The *Statistical Account* carried the following:

> There is a woman alive in Carluke at present, who has for
> more than thirty years been occasionally possessed with a
> dumb spirit. When this spirit of dumbness, indeed, leaves her,
> she makes ample amends for her long silence. But she is
> generally seized with it again in a year or two. She then appears
> to have forgot the use of speech; and for years her teeth are so
> fixed together that it is with the utmost difficulty she can receive
> the necessaries of life.

1795
COLONEL ADDRESSED AS POOR
DRUNKEN DEVIL

William Dickson of Kilbucho took command of the 42nd Regiment
of Foot (the Black Watch), one of whose privates was to be flogged
for drunkenness. As the regiment paraded to witness the punishment,
the culprit took his courage into his hands and addressed his colonel
thus: 'Eh, Kilbucho, ye're surely no gaun tae flog a poor drunken devil
like yoursel'?' The consequence was that the miscreant escaped his
punishment.

DEFEATING THE FRENCH WITH OUR
NATIVE LIQUORS

As the wars against Revolutionary France warmed up, John Wilsone,
president of Glasgow's Beefsteak Club, was horrified to witness a
member downing a glass of whisky, rapidly followed by a glass of
brandy. 'Good God, sir!' exclaimed the president. 'What are you
about? You have disgraced yourself, and the club, by putting a fiddling
Frenchman above a sturdy Highlander.' The culprit unsteadily rose to
his feet, poured himself another whisky, and downed it in one. Laying
his hand upon his heart, he declared, 'Brand me not with being a
democrat, sir; for now I've got the Frenchman between two fires!'

GREATER LOVE HATH NO MAN

In Glasgow there was an outbreak of disorder among the Breadalbane Fencibles, arising from some suspected injustice. Several soldiers were imprisoned and threatened with a flogging, but this only served to whip up the anger of their comrades, who rushed the guard-house and released them. The authorities tried to find the ringleaders, but this proved impossible, as a great proportion of the regiment had been directly involved. It seems that a threat of collective punishment prompted several men to step forward and volunteer to take the penalty that might otherwise be inflicted on the whole. These men were taken to Edinburgh Castle, where four were sentenced to death. Three were reprieved, but the fourth man, Alexander Sutherland (or Morland), was shot on Musselburgh Sands.

1797

OUTBREAK OF THE LOUPING AGUE IN FORFARSHIRE

The *Statistical Account* carried the following account of a strange disease:

Twenty or thirty years ago, what is commonly called the *louping ague* greatly prevailed in Forfarshire. This disease, in its symptoms, has a considerable resemblance to *St Vitus' dance.* Those affected with it, when in a paroxysm, often leap or spring in a very surprising manner, whence the disease has acquired its vulgar name. They frequently leap from the floor to what, in cottages, are called the baulks, or those beams by which the rafters are joined together. Sometimes they spring from one to another with the agility of a cat, or whirl round one of them with a motion resembling the fly of a jack. At other times they run, with astonishing velocity, to some partic-ular place out of doors, which they have fixed on in their minds before, and perhaps mentioned to those in company with them, and then drop down quite exhausted. It is said that the clattering of tongs, or any noise of a similar kind, will bring on the fit. This melancholy disorder still makes its appearance; but it is far from being so common as formerly. Some consider it as entirely a nervous affection; others as the effect of worms. In various instances, the latter opinion has been confirmed by facts.

It is possible that the louping ague *was* St Vitus' dance, known to medicine as Sydenham's chorea, a condition characterised by quick uncontrolled jerkings of the face, hands and feet. It affects between one-fifth and one-third of patients with rheumatic fever, and often only occurs some months after the acute stage of the disease.

TOPPING THE ALPS

Barthelemy Faujas de Saint-Fond published his *Travels in England, Scotland and the Hebrides*, in which he recounted his ascent of Ben More on the island of Mull. 'In my journeys among the High Alps,' he breathlessly wrote, 'I never found so much difficulty as here . . .' Indeed, Saint-Fond failed to make the summit, blaming heather, bog and monotonous lavas.

1798
A GENTLE GIANT

(10 January) Death of William Beaucless, or Bookless, schoolmaster in the parish of Hutton, Berwickshire. The *Edinburgh Weekly Journal* recorded:

> He measured, from the crown of his head to his heel, seven feet eight inches . . . His breadth was in proportion to his length; but he was not athletic, nor, upon the whole, healthy. He died under thirty years of age, and a bachelor. Till within these last few years, he appeared ashamed of his height, and contrived to stoop, that the disparity, in that respect, between him and his neighbours might be as little perceived as possible; but latterly he acquired rather more confidence. He was, however, on no occasion ostentatious of his person; and seldom did his delicacy admit of its being made the subject of joke or merriment. The profession of schoolmaster was the summit of his ambition.

MISTRESS NISH, THE MIGHTY NONAGENARIAN

The *Edinburgh Weekly Journal* carried the following report:

> There is living in the parish of Urr [in Kirkcudbrightshire], a woman of the name of Margaret Nish, at the advanced age of ninety; what is very singular, she can support a burden of seven stones weight upon her back, and will walk with it for several miles, with the most apparent ease and freedom.

WATCHING WHICH WAY THE WIND BLOWS

In reaction to the threat felt from Revolutionary France, the government had the previous year introduced the militia system, which many felt was a form of forcible conscription. In 1798 the summons of the local deputy-lieutenants to the men of Cumnock met with a hostile response, and the officers found themselves being pelted with stones.

One of the officers, a local laird called Logan of Logan, turned up late and found himself in the midst of the angry crowd.

'What's the matter?' he enquired of the rioters, carefully concealing his commission. 'What ails ye at them?'

'Oh, they're gaun to mak us sodgers against our will.'

'Are they really?' the laird exclaimed. 'Filthy fellows! Stane them weel, lads, stane them weel!'

And with that he made good his escape.

1799

UNDERTAKER HANGS HANGING JUDGE

Death of Lord Braxfield, the notorious hanging judge and hounder of radicals. He had famously told one eloquent prisoner in the dock, 'Ye'er a very clever chiel, man, but ye wad be nane the waur o' a hanging.' Another political prisoner who claimed that Christ too had been a reformer was told, 'Muckle he made o' that; he was hanget.' After his own death, he was attended only by the undertakers, a man and a boy. In *Memorials of His Time*, Lord Cockburn describes what happened next, as recounted to him by the boy concerned many years later:

When the 'chesting' had been performed, great was the lad's horror and astonishment to see his elder companion draw from his pocket the end of a rope, which he hitched into a noose, and put it round the neck of the corpse. With many an oath he feigned to hang the dead judge, shouting, with ghastly glee, into the listless ear, 'Monie a ane hae ye hangit, ye auld sinner; an' noo ye're hangit yersel', hoo d'ye like it, ye auld devil?'

The NINETEENTH Century

1800

THE BLACK OFFICER SUFFERS A WHITE DEATH

Early in January, Captain John Macpherson of Ballachroan and a few fellow hunters and their dogs tramped up Glen Tromie into the heart of the Cairngorms, in pursuit of deer. They planned to stay in a small bothy at Gaick, a remote spot in the valley floor, set between steep slopes. After a few days of constant snowfall the hunters had still not returned to their families, and so a search party was sent out. Eventually arriving at Gaick through the white and icy wilds, the search party found no trace of either men or bothy. Eventually it dawned on the rescuers what had happened: both the bothy and the hunters within had been entirely overwhelmed by a giant avalanche. The rescuers managed to dig four bodies out of the ruins of the bothy, buried deep under the avalanche debris, but the fifth body was not recovered until the spring. The disaster became known as *Call Ghàdhaig* – 'the Loss of Gaick' – and it was said to be a revenge upon Macpherson for his supposed dealings with the Devil, and for his unscrupulous and deceitful methods of recruiting young men for the army – a sinister reputation that earned him the sobriquet 'the Black Officer'. Over the years, the stories of the dark doings of the Black Officer were more and more elaborated, and it was rumoured, after his body had been recovered from the snow, that 'it required twelve men, with all their force, to keep down the lid of the coffin whilst it was nailed'.

1801

AN OTTOMAN FROM ARGYLL

En route to take on the French in Egypt, the British fleet called in at Marmaris in southwest Turkey, with which Britain was at that time allied. Among the British regiments on board was the 42nd, the Black Watch, who welcomed an Ottoman general of artillery onto their ship. They were considerably shocked when the man, who was in full Turkish costume and with a white beard flowing down to his girdle, addressed them not only in their native tongue, but in their own accent. It turned out that the general was a Campbell from Kintyre, who in his youth had been so upset when a school friend of his had met with a fatal accident while they played together that he had fled abroad and joined the Ottoman army, in which he had served for 40 years. Now he had come to ask for news of his family, and when he saw the Highlanders in his own native dress, he burst into tears.

1803

IMPRESSED

On their Scottish tour, Wordsworth and Coleridge passed through the remote mining village of Wanlockhead in the hills of Dumfriesshire. There they encountered some barefoot urchins, and were astonished to learn that these children not only attended the local school, but were also studying Homer and Virgil in the original.

NOT IMPRESSED

Visiting the Trossachs and Loch Katrine, Wordsworth described the place as 'gloomy', while his companion Coleridge complained that 'the mountains were all too dreary'. The area had to wait till 1810, and the publication of Scott's long poem *The Lady of the Lake*, with its vivid descriptions of the wild landscape hereabouts, to kick-start its local tourist industry, as recorded by Scott's publisher, Robert Cadell:

> Crowds set off to the scenery of Loch Katrine, till then comparatively unknown; and as the book came out just before the season for excursions, every house and inn in that neighbourhood was crammed with a constant succession of visitors.

It was less good news for the man who operated a ferry across Loch Lomond:

> That d—d Sir Walter Scott . . . I wish I had him to ferry over Loch Lomond: I should be after sinking the boat, if I drowned myself into the bargain; for ever since he wrote his Lady of the Lake, as they call it, everybody goes to see that filthy hole Loch Katrine . . . and I have only had two gentlemen to guide all this blessed season.

Coleridge hadn't thought much of Loch Lomond either, commenting that 'Everywhere there is a distressing sense of local unrememberable' ness.'

SWEET CHARITY

Widow Henderson, a Glasgow landlady, together with her associate Mrs Kilpatrick, was charged with having barred her door against one of her lodgers, Mary Brounlie, who was too sick with a fever to find anywhere else to live, and so died on the doorstep. In her defence, Widow Henderson and Mrs Kilpatrick said they were not related to the dead girl, and had given her a bed out of pure charity. Realising that her illness was terminal, they decided to evict her, so as not to be troubled with bearing the expense of her funeral. Widow Henderson was banished from the City of Glasgow for three years, while Mrs Kilpatrick was sentenced to one month's imprisonment, and fined two guineas.

1804

A JUDICIAL THESAURUS

Death of the famously prolix judge Lord Eskgrove. Henry Cockburn said of him that

> never once did he do or say anything which had the slightest claim to be remembered for any intrinsic merit. The value of all his words and actions consisted in their absurdity.

Cockburn cites Eskgrove's judgment on a tailor who had been convicted for stabbing a soldier to death:

> And not only did you murder him, whereby he was bereaved of his life, but you did thrust, or push, or pierce, or project, or propel, the lethal weapon through the bellyband of his regimental breeches, which were His Majesty's!

1805

NAPOLEON, SCOURGE OF GOD

As French forces massed along the Channel coast ready to invade Britain, Mr Robertson of Kilmarnock preached before the Associate Synod in Glasgow. He told his audience that the probable French invasion would be God's way of chastising the sins of the nation, explaining that Providence was not always nice in the choice of instruments for punishing the wickedness of men. He continued:

> Tak an example frae among yoursels. Your magistrates dinna ask certificates o' character for their public executioners. They generally select sic clamjamfrie as hae rubbit shouthers wi' the gallows themsels. And as for this Bonyparte, I've tell'd ye, my freens, what was the beginning o' that man, and I'll tell ye what will be the end o' him. He'll come doon like a pockfu' o' goats' horns at the Broomielaw!

1807

A DOCTOR CALLS

Death of Alexander 'Lang Sandy' Wood, a much loved Edinburgh surgeon, among whose eccentricities was his habit of visiting his patients accompanied by a pet sheep and a raven.

1809

THE GREAT PEDESTRIAN

For a wager of 1,000 guineas Captain Robert Barclay Allardice of Ury in Aberdeenshire walked 1,000 miles in 1,000 hours at Newmarket, completing the distance, according to *The Times*, 'with perfect ease and great spirit, amidst an immense concourse of spectators' – including two dukes and three earls. During the course of his walk he lost 2 st. 4 lb. Known as 'the Great Pedestrian', Captain Barclay walked 51 miles and back twice a week, and would exercise his dogs daily for 20 or more miles. On one occasion in 1802 he walked 64 miles in ten hours, while in 1806, on bad roads, he completed 100 miles in

19 hours. Captain Barclay died in 1854, as a result of being kicked by a horse.

BELL'S BEEZER

Death of Andrew Bell, the Edinburgh engraver. Although only 4 ft 6 in. tall, he insisted on riding the tallest horse in the city, and would dismount with the aid of a stepladder, to the applause of any onlookers. Other aspects of his appearance also drew attention, especially his crooked legs and his enormous nose. If he caught anybody staring at this protuberance, he would put on an even larger nose made from papier mâché. Among his commissions was the illustration of the midwifery article in the early editions of the *Encyclopædia Britannica* (of which he himself was the co-publisher). These included graphic depictions of the relevant parts of the female anatomy, which were credited with boosting sales. So shocked was King George III that he ordered that the offending pages be ripped out of every copy of the *Encyclopædia*.

1811

WASHING THE BRIDE IN WHISKY

When the poet Shelley eloped with Harriet Westbrook to Edinburgh, where they were married, they were so short of money that they were obliged to put up in inferior lodgings. On the wedding night, their landlord knocked on their door, and announced that it was the local custom for the guests to come in, in the middle of the night, and wash the new bride with whisky. 'I immediately,' said Shelley, 'caught up my brace of pistols, and pointing them both at him, said to him, – "I have had enough of your impertinence; if you give me any more of it I will blow your brains out;" on which he ran or rather tumbled down stairs, and I bolted the doors.'

THE CURSE OF THE GENTRIFIERS

With the proceeds from his successful literary career, Sir Walter Scott bought an estate near Melrose and set to work building a grand Scottish baronial mansion for himself and his collection of relics and antiquities. He named the place Abbotsford, so disguising the fact that the farm that previously stood here had a much earthier, if more authentic, name: Clarty Hole. (*Clarty* is Scots for 'mucky', 'filthy'.)

In the previous century a similar gentrification took place after William K. Laurie bought an estate in Kirkcudbrightshire, and called it Laurieston. He did not wish to keep the existing name, which would have meant he would have had to style himself Laird of Clachan-pluck.

A similar fit of pride came over the soap magnate William Lever, who, having acquired Lewis in 1918, went on, the following year, to purchase the South Harris estate. But he disliked the fact that a small fishing port in his new fiefdom went by what he thought of as the undignified name of Obbe (from Gaelic *An T-ob*, 'the creek'). And so the place was renamed Leverburgh in his honour. Lever puffed himself up further on his ennoblement in 1922, taking the presumptuous title Viscount Leverhulme of the Western Isles.

THE ARGYLL MERMAN

(29 October) Before the sheriff-substitute at Campbeltown, a certain John McIsaac gave the following deposition regarding a creature he had seen on the shores of Kintyre:

> The animal upon the whole was between four and five feet long, as near as he could judge . . . it had a head, arms and body down to the middle like a human being, only that the arms were short in proportion to the body which appeared to be about the thickness of that of a young lad, and tapering gradually to the point of the tail . . . for the first time he saw its face, every feature of which he could see distinctly marked, and which, to him, had all the appearance of the face of a human being, with very hollow eyes.

1812

SHEEPY AFREECAWNUS

Death of former Lord Provost Coulter of Edinburgh, a simple but vain man. On one occasion, while replying to a toast to his health, he announced, 'Although I have the body of a stocking weaver, I have the soul of a Sheepy Afreecawnus!' It is thought that Coulter was alluding to the Roman general who finally defeated Hannibal, Scipio Africanus.

1814

THE TRIUMPH OF HOPE OVER EXPERIENCE

(July) The *European Magazine* carried the following report:

> Lately, at Glasgow, Mr H. Cain, aged 84, to Mrs Maxwell, of Clark's Bridge, aged 96. It is the sixth time for the bride-groom, and the ninth time for the bride, being joined in wedlock.

FIVE CENTURIES AFTER
BANNOCKBURN

An intemperate Englishman was heard to observe to a minister of the kirk that 'No man of taste could think of remaining any time in such a country as Scotland.' To which the clergyman replied: 'I'll tak ye to a place no' far frae Stirling whaur thretty thousand o' yer countrymen hae been for five hunder years, and they've nae thocht o' leavin' yet.'

1815

HONOUR PRESERVED AT WATERLOO

(18 June) Sergeant Weir of the Scots Greys had the responsibility of guarding the payroll of the regiment. But at the Battle of Waterloo he requested special dispensation to be allowed go into action with the rest of the regiment. This being granted, Weir entered the fray, but in one of the charges he was mortally wounded. His body was later found on the battlefield. On his forehead the dying man had, in his own blood and with his own finger, written his name. It was supposed that this

was to avert any suspicion that he had run off with the regiment's money.

A survivor of Waterloo, one Corporal Caithness, was later asked if he was not afraid during the battle. 'Afraid? Why, I was in a' the battles o' the Peninsula!' His interlocutor, fearing he had insulted the corporal, explained that he was enquiring whether he had not been afraid of losing the day. 'Na, na, I didna fear that,' Caithness replied. 'I was only afraid we should a' be killed afore we had time to win it.'

Finally, the following epitaph is said to be copied from a gravestone somewhere in Scotland:

Here lies the body of Alexander Macpherson.
He was a very extraordinary person;
He was two yards high in his stocking feet,
And kept his accoutrements very clean and neat;
He was slew
At the Battle of Waterloo;
He was shot by a bullet
Plump through the gullet;
It went in at his throat,
And came out at the back of his coat.

GOD ONLY SPEAKS ENGLISH

After the final defeat of Napoleon, the following conversation between two old women was overheard in Stranraer:

'Was it no a wonderfu' thing that the Breetish were aye victorious ower the French in battle?'

'Not a bit. Dinna ye ken the Breetish aye say their prayers before gaun into battle?'

'But didna the French say their prayers as weel?'

'Hoot! jabbering bodies, wha could understan' them?'

1816

MACNAB AND THE MOUNTAIN DEW

Death of Francis MacNab, 16th Chief of the Clan MacNab, immor-
talised as *The MacNab* in Henry Raeburn's celebrated portrait of 1802,
and known as *Francis Mor* owing to his mighty stature (he stood 6 ft 3
in. in height).

MacNab objected to government interference in what he regarded
as his fiefdom, and was complicit in the distilling and smuggling of
illicit whisky ('mountain dew') in the area round Callander and Loch
Venachar, where he sat on the Bench as a justice of the peace. On one
occasion he is said to have taken pity on a man arrested on a smuggling
charge, and slipped him the key of the storeroom where his confiscated
barrel of whisky was held. When the barrel was produced as evidence
at the man's trial, it was found to contain nothing but water. Feigning
shock, MacNab dismissed the case, and threatened the excisemen with
contempt of court.

On another occasion, MacNab refused to authorise an excise
expedition against a convoy of smugglers believed to be passing
through Killin at night, on the grounds that the area was well known
to be haunted by goblins and fairies.

MacNab was fond of drinking, gambling and womanising (he
never married), and as a consequence of which he lived in constrained
circumstances and died leaving enormous debts. His nephew
Archibald inherited the chiefdom and was obliged to sell the clan lands
and emigrate to Canada.

1817

HELEN BECOMES JOHN

A young woman called Helen Oliver from Saltcoats was working as
a servant-girl at a farm near West Kilbride. Here she took up with a
young ploughman from a neighbouring farm, and the two, who were
frequently seen walking together 'in quiet and sequestered places', were
regarded as lovers. It turned out the ploughman too was a young
woman. Early the following year, Helen returned to her parents' house,
where she helped herself to her brother John's clothes, and walked to

Glasgow. There she passed herself off as John, and learnt the trade of a plasterer. Whenever her gender was discovered, she was obliged to move on, but she readily found work, as she was a skilled artisan. One of the places she lived and worked was Johnstone. 'There,' wrote a contemporary, unable to get his head round the possibility that human sexual identity is various and multiple, 'either for amusement or to prevent suspicion and ensure concealment, she courted a young woman, and absolutely carried the joke so far as to induce the girl to leave her service to be married.' But John was exposed as Helen by a lad from Saltcoats, who recognised her. Helen/John had to move on again, to Kilmarnock. What happened to her/him after that is unknown.

1820

WOMANLY SACRIFICE

During the radical agitations of these times a band of weavers' wives from Paisley vowed, as a demonstration of their opposition to the reactionary government then in power, to abjure tea and all other items subject to excise duty. John Galt recorded what happened next in his novel *The Ayrshire Legatees* (1821):

> In conformity with this, and actuated by the fine frenzy of the time, they seized their teapots, and marching with them in procession to the bridge, sacrificed them to the goddess of reform, by dashing them, with uplifted arms and intrepid energy, into the river; and afterwards ratified their solemn vows with copious libations of smuggled whisky.

1821

THE LIZARD WITHIN THE STONE

A mason called David Virtue was surprised, when splitting open a large piece of rock from the quarry at Cullaloe in Fife, to find a small lizard embedded in the stone. He was even more surprised when, after a few minutes, the lizard came to life. He reported that it was about an inch and a quarter in length, 'of a brownish yellow colour, and had a round head, with bright sparkling, projecting eyes'. The hollow within the rock bore an exact impression of the creature. The rock had been dug out from deep within the ground, and there was no fissure through which the lizard could have made its entry. Having been liberated from its prison, it ran around for about half an hour, until the mason saw fit to brush it off the rock and kill it.

1822

THE KING'S LAST ENEMY

During George IV's visit to Scotland, an ancient Jacobite veteran of the Battle of Culloden called Patrick Grant was presented to the king in Holyroodhouse. The man introduced himself to the king as 'the last of his enemies'. The king was pleased enough to award Grant a pension for the remaining two years of his life. When Grant died in 1824, aged 111, three pipers accompanied him to his grave, playing some favourite Jacobite tunes.

A TALENT FOR CRUDE PERSONAL ABUSE

(27 March) Sir Alexander Boswell, the son of Dr Johnson's biographer, died of a wound he had received in a duel the previous day. A reactionary Tory, Boswell had purchased a seat in Parliament for the fee of £1,000 per session. He opposed any measure of parliamentary reform, which he believed was against the interests of Scottish landowners. Despite loyally voting for the Tory government, he was disappointed that the prime minister, Lord Liverpool, continued to ignore him, and his grievance intensified when Liverpool refused to award him a baronetcy. Facing financial difficulties, Boswell decided he could no longer afford £1,000 per session, and in 1821 resigned his

seat. A few months later he was awarded his baronetcy, for 'supporting his Majesty's ministers in difficult times'.

Boswell had a talent for crude personal abuse, which he directed at his political enemies, the Whigs. A particular target was James Stuart of Dunearn, whom he anonymously vilified in the pages of *The Beacon* and *The Sentinel*. These attacks steadily became 'not only more frequent, but more personal and virulent', and included a song 'most offensive and most injurious to his character . . . conveying a charge of cowardice'. Having established the identity of his abuser, Stuart insisted on an apology, and when this was not forthcoming issued a challenge. The two met at Auchtertool, near Kirkcaldy. Boswell fired wide, but Stuart, who had never before handled a pistol, found his mark.

Stuart was charged with murder, but was ably defended by his fellow Whig, the noted advocate Henry (later Lord) Cockburn. Regarding the deceased, Cockburn described how

> unfortunately he possessed a gift, often a very fatal one, which gave him an uncommon facility of holding up his adversary to censure or to ridicule. This he had too successfully employed on the present occasion.

Cockburn continued:

> With respect to Mr James Stuart, he should prove him to be of an unimpeachable character; and he affirmed that the rank which he held in society, forced him, as it did many others, to appeal to the laws of honour, when no other tribunal on earth could afford satisfaction.

A succession of favourable character witnesses persuaded the judge that Stuart had acted entirely without malice, and the jury duly returned a verdict of 'not guilty'. According to the court report, 'The verdict was received with loud cheers from without the doors, and with marked approbation from those within.'

Somewhat ironically, in 1819 Boswell – who left debts of £72,000 – had succeeded in having two old Scottish laws against duelling repealed.

1827

A PAROCHIAL MINISTER

Sir Walter Scott noted in his journal that the minister of Great and Little Cumbrae in the Firth of Clyde offered the following prayer:

> Oh Lord, bless and be gracious to the Greater and the Lesser Cumbrays, and in thy mercy do not forget the adjacent islands of Great Britain and Ireland.

'THE SCOTCH, AS A NATION, ARE PARTICULARLY DISAGREEABLE'

The English essayist William Hazlitt offered the following disobliging opinion of Scotland and the Scots in the *Monthly Magazine*:

> Among ourselves, the Scotch, as a nation, are particularly disagreeable. They hate every appearance of comfort themselves, and refuse it to others. Their climate, their religion and their habits are equally averse to pleasure. Their manners are either distinguished by a fawning sycophance (to gain their own ends, and conceal their natural defects), that makes one sick; or by a morose, unblending callousness, that makes one shudder.

1828

THE DAY IT RAINED FISH

Major Forbes Mackenzie of Fodderty, in Ross-shire, was astonished to find while out walking one spring morning that one of his fields was blanketed with the fry of herring, each young fish measuring between three and four inches in length.

1830

THE STONED MERMAID OF BENBECULA

It was reported that the body of a small mermaid was washed up on the shores of Benbecula in the Outer Hebrides. Apparently the creature had been fatally injured by a local boy throwing stones. The local sheriff saw that the body was properly buried, but there was no funeral service. Although the island has both Catholic and Protestant inhabitants, it was presumably not possible in the case of a mermaid to determine whether she kicked with the left or the right foot.

1832

NOTHING HAPPENED

A house in Culross, Fife, bears a sign with the following legend: 'In 1832 on this spot nothing happened.'

1835

REFUSAL TO FIGHT DUEL JUDGED A
MARK OF INSANITY

A Quaker preacher called Catherine Watson visited the small Shetland island of Papa Stour. There she encountered the Hon. Edwin Lindsay, an officer in the Indian army who had been confined on the island since 1809 by his father, Alexander Lindsay, 6th Earl of Balcarres. The Earl had concluded his son was insane after he had refused a challenge to fight a duel. The preacher took pity on the prisoner, finding him neither 'mischievous nor insane', and wrote to his brother, the 7th Earl, to inform him of the case, and to beg for his release. She received no reply. But with the assistance of Captain George Pilkington it was arranged for the Hon. Edwin to be brought before the sheriff of the islands, who agreed that there were no legal grounds for his detention.

On attaining his freedom, the Hon. Edwin wrote to the newspapers to describe how he had been 'struck, maltreated and abused' by his keeper. His supporters explained why he had refused to fight the duel:

. . . he did not feel disposed to rush into the presence of the Almighty, merely to satisfy the splenetic feelings of a military martinet; nor did he himself desire to send a fellow creature to his last account unprepared . . .

Travelling to London with the preacher, the Hon. Edwin went to court to secure the 'small patrimony' to which he believed he was entitled, and in this he was successful. After his liberation, it transpired that his twin brother Richard had also been incarcerated on one of the remoter Orkney islands, allegedly dying 'in a state of complete imbecility'. But there was no inquest. The Hon. Edwin himself lived on for another 30 years.

1840
THE GHOST BIRD OF ST KILDA

The last great auk in the British Isles was captured on St Kilda. The locals thought it was a ghost, and blamed it for the poor weather they had been experiencing. So they killed it and buried it under a pile of stones.

1842
DANGEROUS DRIVING IN THE GORBALS

The Dumfriesshire blacksmith Kirkpatrick Macmillan, known as 'Daft Pate' by his neighbours, and remembered by us as the inventor of the bicycle, pedalled all the way to Glasgow. There, travelling at a reckless 8 mph through the Gorbals, he knocked down a small girl. Although she was only grazed, Macmillan was arrested and brought before the magistrate. The latter fined him five shillings (although he may have paid the fine himself, so struck was he by Macmillan's invention). The press was more cynical, opining that 'This invention will not supersede the railway.'

1844

ALLART'S HAPPY FAMILY

The exhibit so-named was put on show at No. 63 Princes Street, Edinburgh, an advertisement advising the public that said happy family consisted

> of upwards of 100 ANIMALS, of an Opposite Nature, *All Living and Feeding in One Apartment*. The following are a few of the Collection, namely Rats, Cats, Ferret, Coatimundi, Squirrel, Hawks, Owls, Pigeons, Crows, Jackdaws, Magpies, Starlings, Blackbirds, Chickens, Monkeys, Hedgehog, Sea-Gull, Guinea Pigs, Goose, Parrots, &c, &c too numerous to mention. *Most wonderful to see how they all agree in one large cage.*

BOSJEMANS EAT LIVE RATS IN GLASGOW

Meanwhile, Glasgow flocked to an entertainment featuring 'Bosjemans' – i.e. Bushmen from southern Africa. Although nearly 100,000 people paid a penny per head to watch the show, it was rumoured that the Bosjemans were actually Irish labourers dressed in skins and feathers, and that their incomprehensible utterances were in fact Gaelic. The high point of the performance seems to have been the consumption of live rats by one of the players.

1845

ACADEMIC DOES FOR FAIRIES

The *New Statistical Account* of Scotland records that a late Principal of Aberdeen University had contributed 'by his benevolent exertions in an eminent degree to the expulsion of fairies from the Highland Hills'.

1847

SURGEON INADVERTENTLY REMOVES MAN'S TESTICLES

(7 December) Death of the Edinburgh-trained surgeon Robert Liston, known as 'the Great Northern Anatomist'. In the age before anaesthesia his speed with the scalpel and the bone saw were highly valued, and he would encourage his watching students to time him on their pocket watches. On one occasion he amputated a man's leg in two and a half minutes, although he inadvertently also removed the man's testicles at the same time. The patient later died of hospital gangrene, as did Liston's assistant, who lost his fingers to the surgeon's scalpel during the same frenzied operation. To cap it all, Liston in his haste somehow slashed the coat of a fellow surgeon who was observing the proceedings, and who, convinced that he had been stabbed, promptly died of fright.

EAST−WEST RIVALRY

Following the Ordnance Survey measurements establishing that Ben Nevis and not Ben Macdui was Britain's highest mountain, the Earl of Fife, on whose land that latter hill was located, declared that he was to be buried on its summit under a vast cairn that would take its height from 4,295 feet to something in excess of Ben Nevis's 4,406 feet. The plan was never put into action.

1848

A DOSE OF THE WRONG SALTS

(14 June) Death of Donald Robertson, at the age of 63. The inscription on his gravestone in Eshaness, Shetland, reads:

> He was a peaceable, quiet man, and to all appearances a sincere Christian. His death was much regretted which was caused by the stupidity of Laurence Tulloch of Clothister (Sullom) who sold him nitre instead of Epsom Salts by which he was killed in the space of five hours after taking a dose of it.

1850

A 'GOOD-HUMOURED FROLIC' IN LINLITHGOW

Sir William Don, whose profligacy had lost him his inherited fortune and obliged him to pursue a career on the stage, appeared at Linlithgow Sheriff Court. There he faced three charges: one of malicious mischief, one of wanton and reckless mischief, and one of breach of the peace. This embarrassing circumstance arose from the events of the night of 29–30 November the previous year, following the dinner of the Linlithgow and Stirlingshire Hunt at the Star and Garter in Linlithgow. After leaving the inn, Sir William and several of his equally well-refreshed friends – including Sir John Dick Lauder, Professor Lizars, Captain Stirling Stewart, Lord Gilbert Kennedy, Mr Ramsay of Barton and Sir Alexander Gibson Maitland of Cliftonhall – made their way to the station to catch the Edinburgh train.

The station master, a Mr Young, was alerted to their arrival by the sound of breaking glass. Mr Young was then confronted by a number of gentlemen demanding tickets, and while he was attending to them, Captain Stewart vaulted over the counter, extinguished a gas lamp, and started to play with the telegraph wires. On being requested by Mr Young to desist, the Captain threatened to beat him with his cane, although all he managed to do was to rattle the official's hat with a ruler. At this point, Sir William barged into the back office, extinguishing another light. This inspired his friends to play a game involving turning off every lamp they could find, while singing at the tops of their voices. Mr Young and a number of porters rushed around after them attempting to re-light the lamps. While this was going on, Sir William started fiddling with the telegraph, turning the handles and ringing the bell. By this time the floor was strewn with broken glass, torn notices and a number of boiled potatoes that Sir William had pocketed at the Star and Garter.

At this point, Lord Kennedy demanded that Mr Young sell him a ticket. The latter requested that His Lordship be patient, while they lit the lamps. Patience was a virtue lacking at this moment in Lord Kennedy, who promptly struck Mr Young over the head with his cane. Mr Young grabbed the cane, and turned it on his erstwhile assailant.

Showing considerable initiative, one of the porters, a Mr Masterton, went out onto the platform and rang the hand bell to indicate that the train was approaching. At this signal, all the gentlemen rushed onto the platform, while Masterton dodged back inside, and locked the door. Masterton had tricked them, and the gentlemen were obliged to wait for ten minutes in the cold for the actual arrival of the train, their barrage of shouting and hammering on the locked door having failed to move the station staff to relent. When the train *did* arrive, the gentlemen piled aboard, taking with them the hand bell. Mr Young requested its return, explaining that the train could not depart unless he rang it. His request was met with 'an extraordinary volley of oaths', amounting to a refusal.

Nevertheless, no doubt to Mr Young's relief, the train did depart, and the gentlemen (with the exception of Professor Lizars, who slept throughout) then set about vandalising the two compartments that they occupied. By the time they reached Edinburgh and alighted, the guard, William Bassett, found that many of the fittings – including rugs, curtains, brass rods and straps – had been thrown out of the window.

At this point Sir John Dick Lauder returned to the platform, and asked the guard if he had seen his hat (presumably having failed to notice that his companions had thrown it out of the window, along with all the fittings). Bassett said that in view of the damage, he would have to detain Sir John until he received further orders, and blocked his attempt to escape. Two policemen at Waverley Station declined to become involved, as the damage had been perpetrated outwith their jurisdiction. However, when Sir John took Bassett by the lapels and began to shake him, one of the policemen interposed his body, round which Sir John attempted to land kicks and punches on the unfortu-nate guard, who later testified that three punches had reached their mark, while a boot had struck him in the groin, resulting in a feeling of nausea that had persisted for two hours.

The upshot was that some weeks later Sir John found himself before the Sheriff Court in Edinburgh, and was found guilty of assault. The Sheriff said that, in passing sentence, he had a difficult task, as he had known Sir John since infancy. He gave him a choice: pay a fine of £10, or spend 20 days behind bars. Sir John opted for the fine.

Sir William got off even more lightly at his trial in Linlithgow.

He alone was chosen to face the charges, as he was deemed to be by far the soberest of the gentlemen involved. His defence counsel described the evening's events as merely a 'good-humoured frolic', and after weighing all the evidence the jury returned a verdict of 'not proven' on all three charges. The Sheriff was, he confessed, thus relieved of the 'very painful' duty of handing down a sentence on the young baronet. He was, however, obliged to issue an admonishment, and he duly told Sir William that he hoped that his conduct in future might never again 'place him in such a position as he had occupied that day'.

Sir William continued his career on the stage, and in later life specialised in taking female comic roles. He died suddenly in 1862 of an aortic aneurysm while touring Tasmania with a burlesque of *Kenilworth*, in which he played the part of Queen Elizabeth I.

1851
THE COW OF PROPHECY

Having fallen into ruin, Fairburn Tower, between Muir of Ord and Strathpeffer, was used by a local farmer to store hay. One day one of his cows followed a trail of hay up the stairs of the tower, but then became stuck at the top. Unable to descend, the unfortunate creature was obliged to give birth to a calf in this lofty location, thus, it was widely said, fulfilling one of the prophecies of the Brahan Seer:

> The day will come when the MacKenzies of Fairburn shall lose their entire possessions; their castle will become uninhabited and a cow shall give birth to a calf in the uppermost chamber of the tower.

The Brahan Seer, also known as Coinneach Odhar, was a somewhat murky figure who was said to have offered many predictions about the future in the 16th or 17th centuries, although his historical reality is uncertain.

The farmer kept the cow atop the tower for five days, charging visitors to witness this prodigious event.

1852

A DUCAL PEACOCK

(18 August) Death of Alexander Hamilton, 10th Duke of Hamilton. At the age of 15 he had been painted by Joshua Reynolds with long hair and open-necked lacy shirt, and his subsequent career gave him many opportunities to dress up, his posts and honorifics including Ambassador to the Court of St Petersburg, Lord Lieutenant of Lanarkshire, Lord High Steward at the coronations of William IV and Victoria, Knight of the Garter, Hereditary Keeper of Holyroodhouse and Grand Master of the Freemasons in Scotland.

After Hamilton's death an obituary noted that 'timidity and variableness of temperament prevented his rendering much service to, or being much relied on by his party [the Whigs] . . . With a great predisposition to over-estimate the importance of ancient birth . . . he well deserved to be considered the proudest man in England'. Indeed, such was his family pride that he considered himself, as the descendant of the Regent Arran, as the rightful heir to the throne of Scotland. A contemporary remembered that even in old age the Duke 'was always dressed in a military laced undress coat, tights and Hessian boots, &c', while another acquaintance remarked on how his fingers were covered in gold rings.

The Duke prepared for his own death well in advance. In 1836 he had acquired an ancient Egyptian sarcophagus ostensibly for the British Museum but in fact for his own interment, while in 1842 he began the construction of the immense and grandiose Hamilton Mausoleum. In accordance with his wishes, his body was mummified after death, but when it came to placing him in the sarcophagus, a difficulty arose. The Duke was of considerably greater stature than the princess for whom the sarcophagus had originally been made, so it was found necessary to cut off His Grace's feet and place them beside him in his grave.

1853

LAIRD PREVENTS PROFANATION OF SABBATH BY DAY-TRIPPERS

(22 August) Day-trippers from Glasgow attempting to disembark from the paddle steamer *Emperor* at the resort of Garelochhead were informed by the local laird, Sir James Colquhoun, that they could not do so, as it was a Sunday. The day-trippers were inclined to ignore this prohibition, so Sir James ordered his keepers to prevent the disembarkation by force. There was something of a ruckus, ending in a defeat for the righteous. However, Sir James took the matter to the courts, who banned cruises on the Sabbath for a number of years.

1854

AN ARITHMETICAL PRODIGY

The *North British Daily Mail* carried an account of an astonishing arithmetical prodigy. This was the eight- or nine-year-old Margaret Cleland, daughter of a shoemaker in Darvel, Ayrshire. Her rapidity in mental calculation astonished her teacher and her classmates alike. Two of the latter reported how, for the bet of a penny, she had multiplied 123,456,789 by 987,654,321 in less than half a minute (they had laboriously checked her answer). She, however, refused to accept her winnings.

1859

THE SPEECH THAT NEVER WAS

(25 January) On Burns Night in the poet's centennial year, John Stuart Blackie, translator of Goethe's *Faust* and Professor of Greek at Edinburgh University, was asked to make a speech. Seeing that he was to be the last speaker of the evening, he was inclined to refuse the invitation, given that no one would listen to him, for the company would be tired and in its cups by then. But he was reassured that his every word would be attended upon. A grand speech, he was told, was required for such a grand occasion, so he must 'build it up architecturally, like Cicero, Demosthenes, and the orators of old'. Blackie himself picks up the story:

Like a good-natured fellow as I was, I wrote out a long speech. Well, at the dinner, people soon got tired, and the most eloquent men were not listened to. When it came to my turn I saw there was no chance; so I merely said, 'I propose so and so; goodbye,' and sat down. But next day, there in all the papers was the great speech that I had never delivered a word of – not only a whole column of type, but sprinkled with 'hear-hears', 'hurrahs' and all that sort of thing. It was the greatest lie that ever was printed; and you will find it there, making me immortal to the end of the world, wherever the name of Burns is known.

Professor Blackie never wrote down a speech again in his lifetime, preferring to speak extempore whenever called upon.

1861

WE ARE NOT AMUSED

(8 October) Queen Victoria stayed the night at the inn at Dalwhinnie, and was less than pleased. 'Unfortunately there was hardly anything to eat,' she wrote in her journal, 'and there was only tea, and two miserable starved Highland chickens, without any potatoes! No pudding, and no fun!'

PLUCK

(24 November) One of the rickety old tenements that lined the High Street of Edinburgh collapsed, causing the deaths of 35 people. The only survivor was a boy called Joseph McIvor. Trapped under the rubble, he kept up the spirits of his rescuers with the adjuration, 'Heave awa, lads, I'm no deid yet.' The building that was constructed on the site the following year became known as 'Heave Awa House'.

1864

THE LAST PUBLIC HANGING

George Bryce, 'the Ratho Murderer', achieved the dubious distinction of becoming the last man to be hanged in public in Edinburgh. He had slit the throat of a nursemaid called Jane Seton, who had advised her fellow servant Isabella Brown to break off her affair with Bryce before her reputation was ruined. Bryce, who was known to be 'simple', was hanged on the Lawnmarket before a jeering crowd of 26,000 people. The execution did not go according to plan, however, as the hangman, who had been drafted in from York, miscalculated the length of rope required. As a consequence, Bryce's neck was not instantly broken, and instead he took some 40 minutes to die by slow strangulation. This turned the crowd's wrath against the hapless hangman, who required police protection. Thereafter the Edinburgh authorities declared that in future all executions should be conducted behind closed doors. Today a pub close to the site bears a memorable name: The Last Drop.

1865

END OF THE WORLD PREDICTED – AGAIN

Charles Piazzi Smyth, the Astronomer Royal for Scotland, conducted detailed measurements of the Great Pyramid at Giza in Egypt. He concluded that it was designed using a unit he called the 'pyramid-inch', equal to 1.001 British inches and based on the biblical cubit. He also asserted that the architect of the Great Pyramid must have been an Old Testament patriarch, perhaps the priest Melchizedek, who had been guided by God. The inch being therefore divinely ordained, Piazzi Smyth was confirmed in his fervent opposition to an official proposal made in 1864 to introduce the metric system into the UK – for was not the metre and all its kin the spawn of atheistical French radicals? In his researches, Piazzi Smyth found many 'significant' measurements in the structure of the Great Pyramid: for example, the perimeter of the base measured 365,000 inches, 1,000 times the number of days in the year, while the height of the pyramid in inches bore a numerical relationship to the distance to the Sun measured in miles. Piazzi Smyth believed that embedded in these and other measurements, numbers and ratios were a collection of prophecies, including a prediction that the world would come to an end in 1881. When this failed to occur, he issued a succession of alternative dates. The Royal Society declined to publish his paper on the matter, and this and other disappointments led to his resignation as Astronomer Royal for Scotland in 1888.

1866
THE DEVIL'S SHARE

The belief that the soul of the first corpse to be buried in a new graveyard would be taken by the Devil caused problems when a new site was opened in Aberdeenshire. Quite simply, the locals refused to bury their dead there. The difficulty was resolved when a tramp was found dead on the road. As no one claimed him, he was duly interred. Thereafter, people were quite happy to be buried in the new graveyard, confident that their souls would be safe.

1868
A CURE FOR MADNESS

It was claimed that a 'madman' was cured after some ancient rituals were performed on Isle Maree in Loch Maree. St Maree or Maelrubha had become conflated with the old Celtic god Mourie, and on the island there is a well and a tree sacred to this local deity. The rituals, performed from time immemorial, involve offerings of milk, sacrifices of bulls, and the insertion of coins into the bark of the tree. This last tradition was upheld by Queen Victoria when she visited the island in 1877.

1872
DRUNK IN CHARGE OF A COW

The Licensing Act made it an offence to be intoxicated while in charge of a cow, horse or steam engine in Scotland.

1873

THE RIGHT TO ROAM

Death of William Dobson of Galashiels, a man certain of his rights. One day, while he walked in Gala Parks, he was hailed by the laird, who demanded what right he had to be there. 'Od, man,' replied Dobson, 'I hae walkit here lang afore ye was born, and was never found faut wi', and I'm no gaun to be stoppit noo.'

1879

A REMNANT OF BELIEF IN WITCHCRAFT

A man in Dingwall was sent to prison for attacking an old woman he claimed was a witch. He had concluded that he could only break the curse he believed she had placed upon his fishing boat – which as a consequence failed to land any fish – if he shed her blood.

1880

MANY A TRUE WORD . . .

Grand Duke Alexis of Russia visited Scotland to attend the launch of the steam yacht *Livadia*, which had been commissioned by Tsar Alexander II. In the course of his speech at the John Elder yard in Govan, Grand Duke Alexis described Glasgow as 'the centre of the intelligence of England'.

1884

HIGH DUDGEON

Two men from Lewis, having fallen out with their local minister, set sail for the small, remote island of North Rona. The last inhabitant, a shepherd, had left the island 40 years before, the place having been devastated by an invasion of rats in the 17th century. Within a year the exiles from Lewis were both dead.

1887

HIGHLY DEVELOPED BREASTS OBSERVED
IN LOCH MORAR

This year saw the first sighting of 'Morag', a monster supposed to haunt Loch Morar, Scotland's deepest loch. Numerous sightings have subse-quently been reported. In some accounts the creature is something like a mermaid, with flowing hair and 'highly developed breasts'; in others it is a 'black heap or ball' presaging the death of a local, possibly by drowning. In a 1948 report it was described as a 'peculiar serpent-like creature, about 20 feet long'.

The closest encounter came at about 9 p.m. on 16 August 1969. Duncan McDonnel and William Simpson had been having a day on the loch. McDonnel was at the wheel of their motor boat, and later described what he saw:

> I heard a splash or disturbance in the water astern of us. I looked up and saw about twenty yards behind us this creature coming directly after us in our wake. It only took a matter of seconds to catch up with us. It grazed the side of the boat, I am quite certain this was unintentional. When it struck the boat seemed to come to a halt or at least slow down. I grabbed the oar and was attempting to fend it off, my one fear being that if it got under the boat it might capsize it.

Simpson added his account:

> As we were sailing down the loch in my boat we were suddenly disturbed and frightened by a thing that surfaced behind us. We watched it catch us up then bump into the side of the boat, the impact sent a kettle of water I was heating onto the floor. I ran into the cabin to turn the gas off as the water had put the flame out. Then I came out of the cabin to see my mate trying to fend the beast off with an oar, to me he was wasting his time. Then when I seen the oar break I grabbed my rifle and quickly putting a bullet in it fired in the

direction of the beast. I watched it slowly sink away from the boat and that was the last I seed of it.

The creature had by this time grown to some 25 or 30 feet, and possessed three humps and a head said to have been a foot wide.

1891
THE LOCHABER MATTERHORN

A correspondent wrote to the *Glasgow Herald* bemoaning the fact that Ben Nevis, Britain's highest mountain, was so lacking in distinction in terms of shape. Indeed, from most directions the Ben appears to be no more than a flat-backed lump. To remedy this, the correspondent suggested that vast amounts of rock be dynamited from neighbouring peaks and piled on top of the Ben 'to form a more lofty and graceful summit to the hill, bringing it to the full height of 5,000 feet, and giving the British tourist a finer mountain to look at and to ascend; the view would be superb'. Happily, the Ben was saved from being turned into a slag heap by the indifference of the public.

1892
OUR LOST LAUREATE

On the death of the poet laureate Alfred, Lord Tennyson, the Dundee rhymester William McGonagall walked 60 miles in the rain to Balmoral, intending to ask Queen Victoria to appoint him to the recently vacated post. He had, he claimed, penned much fine royal verse, such as 'An Ode to the Queen on her Jubilee Year':

> And as this is her first Jubilee year,
> And will be her last, I rather fear:
> Therefore, sound drums and trumpets cheerfully,
> Until the echoes are heard o'er land and sea.

On his arrival at Balmoral, he was informed Her Majesty was not in residence.

The
TWENTIETH
Century *and*
Beyond

1900
FARMER BEHOLDS MERMAID OF RAVISHING BEAUTY

(5 January) While tending to his sheep in remote Sandwood Bay in Sutherland, a local farmer, Alexander Gunn, had an uncanny experience. His friend, MacDonald Robertson, recounted what Gunn had told him:

> Gunn's collie suddenly let out a howl and cringed in terror at his feet. On a ledge, above the tide, a figure was reclining on the rock face. At first he thought it was a seal, then he saw the hair was reddish-yellow, the eyes greenish-blue and the body yellowish and about 7 ft long. To the day Alexander Gunn died in 1944, his story never changed and he maintained that he had seen a mermaid of ravishing beauty.

THE MYSTERY OF THE FLANNAN ISLES

The only inhabitants of the remote Flannan Isles, far out to sea west of Lewis, were the three lighthouse keepers. On Boxing Day 1900 the Northern Lights vessel *Hesperus* arrived from Oban, having been delayed several days by severe storms. When the relief party landed they could find no sign of any of the three keepers. There were notes for the log up to 15 December, the kitchen was tidy apart from one chair lying on its side, and the lamp was ready to be lit. Two sets of oilskins were missing from their pegs by the door. The door and the gate beyond were both closed.

The official investigation concluded that all three men must have gone to the west landing (where the investigator found considerable damage) to secure some gear. Here, he concluded, they had been overwhelmed by a huge wave breaking over them and sweeping them out to sea. But why would one of the men have gone out without his oilskins in such weather? The mystery has led to much wild speculation. Had one keeper gone mad and murdered the other two? Perhaps a sea serpent had snatched them from the shore? Had foreign spies abducted them? A more prosaic explanation may be that the third keeper, knowing that the west landing was vulnerable to huge breakers, had spotted some massive waves heading that way and rushed out to warn his two companions. But why, in that case, had he taken the time to close the door and the gate?

1902

JUDGES DECRY PROSPECT OF SCOTLAND BEING DOTTED WITH MONUMENTS TO OBSCURE PERSONS

Death of the banker, businessman and philanthropist John Stuart McCaig, the son of a farmer from Lismore. He had prepared for his eventual demise by designing McCaig's Tower, a circular structure resembling the Colosseum in Rome, with a diameter of 200 metres, to be built on top of a hill overlooking Oban. The intention was to provide a monument to himself and his family, and in the process to give work to local stonemasons through the winter months. In his will McCaig specified precisely what he wanted: on top of the wall of the tower were to be erected giant bronze statues of his mother, father, five brothers and four sisters. These would provide work for Scottish sculptors, who were to base the likenesses on photographs, and where these were unavailable for any of his relatives, the sculptors were to use one of McCaig himself. Construction began in 1897.

After his death, McCaig's will was challenged by his surviving sibling Catherine, and the Court of Session duly ruled that the Tower was self-advertisement, and was therefore not charitable in purpose. Strangely enough, Catherine's own will after she died in 1913 specified that the statues of herself, her parents and her siblings *should* be erected after all. Her will in turn was challenged, and in 1915 the Court of Session considered the case, which was gleefully reported in the *Scotsman*:

> The Lord Justice Clerk said it was a good thing it was limited to statues and not to obelisks such as were set up. These things were monstrous ... They could be seen fifty miles away. It would be useful if Zeppelins would come and knock them down.

There was some debate as to how to treat the proposed statue of McCaig's brother Peter, who had died in infancy around three-quarters of a century earlier. To deal with this problem, the Lord Justice Clerk suggested 'that they could get a prize baby to copy from'. He went on to suggest that 'Mr McCaig might look splendid in a Roman toga', to which the Dean of the Faculty responded: 'Our own statesmen are always enveloped in a toga which they never wore. They would have been taken up for indecent exposure if they had.' Lord Guthrie added, 'If the statues were put in, the place would be called "McCaig's Folly."' To which the Lord Justice Clerk replied, 'It is called that already.'

On 21 January 1915 their lordships delivered their verdict. Lord Salvesen's views were reported as follows:

> The expenditure of this large sum on statues, which was directed apparently from motives of personal and family vanity, would serve no purpose, all the more seeing that the family had virtually become extinct. It could not be of benefit to the public, because the enclosure in which the statues were to be erected was one to which they would have no right of access . . . The prospect of Scotland being dotted with monuments to obscure persons who happened to have amassed a sufficiency of means, and cumbered with trusts for the purpose of maintaining these monuments in all time coming, appeared to his Lordship to be little less than appalling.

For his part, Lord Guthrie opined:

> The statues would not, in fact, achieve Miss McCaig's object of perpetuating an honourable memory. They would turn a respectable and creditable family into a laughing-stock to succeeding generations.

The Lord Justice Clerk agreed, saying 'that with reference to a remark made by Lord Guthrie, where he spoke of a testator ordering his money to be thrown into the sea, he thought such an order might be more rational than the orders given to the trustees in this case'.

Nevertheless, the Court of Session approved the establishment of the Catherine McCaig Trust, intended to promote the use of the Gaelic language. The Tower itself, devoid of statuary, now encloses a public garden, providing splendid views out towards some of the Inner Hebrides.

1910
POSSIBLE SIGHTING OF THE NUGGLE OFF ORKNEY

While out shooting ducks in Shapinsay Sound off Orkney Mainland, a man saw a sea monster with an 18-foot neck and the head of a horse. This may have been the Nuggle, or Noggelvi, the Orkney and Shetland version of the Celtic Kelpie.

1920
BLUE WHALE PUTREFIES OFF COAST OF LEWIS

(September) A blue whale was found on the shores of Lewis, stuck in some rocks. How the unfortunate beast had found its way this far north from its customary habitat in the Southern Ocean is unclear, but there was a harpoon sticking out of its back. The remains, now in an advanced state of decay, were towed to Bragar Bay, to await the pleasure of His Majesty – all whales being 'royal fish'. No decision being forthcoming from the powers that be, the villagers found themselves increasingly troubled by the stench, and eventually took the initiative by towing the putrid innards out to sea and harvesting the valuable blubber. The local postmaster created an arch out of the lower jawbone, which still stands. The harpoon, much to everybody's surprise, suddenly detonated while it was being polished in a garage, and blew a hole in the wall. It was subsequently incorporated as the centrepiece of the jawbone archway.

1921
INVERNESS BECOMES SEAT OF IMPERIAL POWER

(7 September) For the first time ever, the British Cabinet met outside London – in Inverness. This unlikely choice of venue was dictated by the fact that Lloyd George was holidaying in Gairloch at the time, and summoned an emergency meeting to discuss the crisis in Ireland.

1922

EIGHT SUFFER DEATH BY DUCK PASTE

Tragedy struck the Loch Maree Hotel, a place popular with anglers. Eight people – both guests and gillies – died in mysterious circum stances. After an extensive investigation, it was established that all of the victims had on the same day (14 August) eaten duck paste sandwiches. The duck paste in question turned out to have been contaminated by the bacterium *Clostridium botulinum*, the cause of the disease called botulism (from Latin *botulus*, 'sausage' – sausages being prone to contamination with the microbe in question). Botulism is characterised by progressive failure of the nervous system, leading to loss of control over eye movements, speech, chewing and swallowing, followed by weakness of the limbs, and, in severe cases, respiratory failure. There is no fever, and the patient is aware of what is happening throughout.

1924

GAME SPOILS SPORT

For centuries, the people of Fortingall in Perthshire had celebrated Halloween on the nearby Càrn nam Marbh ('cairn of the dead'), by tradition the mass grave of locals who had died in the Black Death, but in reality a Bronze Age barrow. In preparation for the festivities the locals would gather large amounts of gorse from the neighbouring hillsides and pile it on top of the barrow. On the night itself, the gorse would be set alight and the villagers would dance around the fire, holding hands. As the flames died down, the young men would dare each other to leap over the smouldering embers. All this came to an end in 1924, when the local gamekeeper, concerned that his birds were being deprived of cover, issued an edict that no more gorse was to be taken from the locality.

1927

SCOTLAND'S LATTERDAY HERMITS

Johnnie Logie took up residence in a cave on Luce Bay, near the Mull of Galloway. For the next 35 years he kept himself comfortable there with the aid of a wood-burning stove and his own rainwater gathering system. He fed himself on potatoes grown in the seaweed he gathered from the shore. Logie only left his cave on two occasions, both times in need of medical attention. 'Oh, I wish I was back in ma ain wee cave,' he told the *Sunday Post*. A year before his death in 1962 he moved out of his cave to spend his last days with relatives in Ayrshire.

The role of Scotland's best-known hermit was taken over by a former soldier, Tom Leppard (né Woodbridge), known as the Leopard Man, as more than 99 per cent of his body is covered with tattooed spots. Leppard lived for many years in a simple home-made bothy near Kyleakin on Skye. Every week he would kayak across the strait to do his shopping and collect his pension in Kyle of Lochalsh. Should he require anything at the chemist, the usual question was whether he needed something to clear up his spots. In 2008, at the age of 73, he retired to sheltered housing in Broadford.

1931

ISLANDERS SALVAGE CONDOMS, A PIANO AND TWO CADILLACS

(July) An American ship, the *Pennsylvania*, got into difficulties in the wild waters of the Pentland Firth, and found itself grounded on rocks off the small island of Stroma. The inhabitants of the island, long skilled in salvage work, set about 'rescuing' the ship's cargo, which included prams, toys, slot-machines, furniture, sewing machines, watches, lingerie, food, tobacco, typewriters, condoms, a piano and two Cadillacs. It wasn't long before the authorities – in the form of customs officials, policemen, coastguards and the Receiver of Wrecks – descended upon the island. But they were no match for the cunning of the islanders, who hid the booty in peat stacks, lochs and caves – even under the font in the church. The women of the island proved adept at diversionary tactics, rushing around with cloth-wrapped bundles, most of which contained innocuous items such as a bag of potatoes or a baby, but some of which contained genuine booty. One of the former inhabitants of the island, which was finally deserted in the 1960s, justified the actions of the 'Stroma Pirates' by explaining that if they had not reached the wreck quickly, all the cargo would have ended up at the bottom of the sea, beyond all hope of salvage.

1932

SHIP GETS INTO TROUBLE ABOVE STRATHPEFFER

An event occurred in the popular spa village of Strathpeffer that was taken to fulfil a troubling prophecy by the Brahan Seer (see 1851): 'A village with four churches will get another spire, and a ship will come from the sky and moor at it.' Tradition took the village to be Strathpeffer, close to Brahan, and there was considerable local opposition in the mid-19th century when it was proposed to build a fifth church, many fearing that it would herald the drowning of the village in some deluge. So there was some relief, and even amusement, when in 1932 an airship got into trouble near the village and was obliged to anchor itself by grappling iron to the spire of the new church.

1933

TOURIST INDUSTRY GIVEN MAJOR BOOST

On 22 July 1933 it was reported that a 'grey monster', some six feet long, had been seen crossing a road near Loch Ness. No such creature had been reported in the vicinity since St Adamnan, in his life of Columba (7th century), had mentioned an *aquatalis bestia* living in Loch Ness. However, after the 1933 sighting the beast was being spotted right, left and centre. It was all excellent news for the local hoteliers, hirers of boats, drivers of charabancs, and so on.

1936

'I OUGHT TO BE KING OF THIS COUNTRY'

Death of Robert Bontine Cunninghame Graham, adventurer, writer and politician, ardent champion of the underdog and one of the most colourful Scots of his age, who in 1934 had become the first president of the Scottish National Party. Cunninghame Graham, whose name reflects his descent from the Cunningham Earls of Glencairn and the Graham Earls of Menteith, was the eldest son of Major William Cunninghame Bontine of the Renfrew Militia and the Hon. Anne Elizabeth Elphinstone-Fleeming, daughter of Admiral Charles Elphinstone-Fleeming and a Spanish noblewoman, Doña Catalina Paulina Alessandro de Jiménez (the birth took place aboard the admiral's flagship off the coast of Venezuela). Through the Earls of Menteith, Cunninghame Graham could trace his ancestry back to Robert II, and indeed his friend Andrew Lang insisted that he should be known as Robert IV of Scotland (and Robert I of Great Britain and Ireland). 'I ought, madam, if I had my rights,' Cunninghame Graham once informed an acquaintance, 'to be king of this country.'

1937

BE GOOD TO YOUR GRANNY AND
GIVE HER PLENTY OF WHISKY

Death of Alexander Wylie Petrie, a colourful Glasgow character who had adopted the byname 'the Clincher', claiming that he possessed one particularly brilliant brain cell, which gave him the power to *clinch* any argument. A hairdresser by trade, from 1897 until his death Petrie wrote, published and sold his own newspaper, *The Glasgow Clincher*, in which he campaigned tirelessly against the Glasgow Establishment, and in particular against what he saw as the inefficiency, prodigality, corruption and vulgarity of Glasgow corporation (the council), telling his readers:

> You Glasgow people, for years and years you have been sending men into the Town Council who have no brains, but then you are a consistent people. You love your neighbours as yourselves.

His constant vexing of the corporation led them to have him arrested and incarcerated in Woodilee Asylum near Lenzie, where they attempted to have him certified insane. However, Petrie had gained the loyalty of his readers, whom he had shamelessly flattered in the pages of his paper with such pronouncements as:

> *The Clincher* has not the largest circulation in Glasgow, but it has the most intellectual readers in the world.

Outraged at his incarceration at Woodilee, his followers raised a public outcry, and ensured that Petrie was examined by an independent doctor, who issued him with a clean bill of mental health. Thereafter Petrie, resplendent in his customary formal suit, top hat and fulsome white beard, would regale passers-by with the boast that he was the only man in Glasgow to be certified sane. Michael Munro, in the 2002 edition of *The Crack: The Best of Glasgow Humour*, relates his own father's memories of the Clincher:

> He always had a kindly word for children, and would invari-
> ably advise my father and his cronies to 'be good to your
> granny and give her plenty of whisky'.

1939
THE LIGHTS HAVE GONE OUT ALL OVER EUROPE

At the first Hogmanay of the Second World War, blackout regulations meant that the citizens of Biggar had to abandon their centuries-old custom of lighting a huge bonfire in the main street of the town. Instead, they gathered round a solitary candle, burning in a tin.

1941
DYNAMITING WHISKY JUDGED CRAZY

(5 February) The SS *Politician* foundered in the Sound of Barra south of Eriskay. It had been carrying a cargo of 264,000 bottles of whisky to the USA, along with 290,000 ten-shilling notes. The islanders set about salvaging as much as they could, but the officers of HM

Customs and Excise were soon on the case, and several men ended up serving prison sentences in Inverness or Peterhead. In the end the authorities blew up the wreck. 'Dynamiting whisky?' exclaimed one witness. 'You wouldn't think there'd be men in the world so crazy as that!' The incident was the basis of Compton Mackenzie's novel *Whisky Galore*, and the film based upon it.

1942
THE SEEDING OF ANTHRAX ISLAND

Government scientists, fearing that the Germans were about to attack Britain with biological weapons, decided to use Gruinard Island in the far northwest of Scotland to test the effects of anthrax. They herded a flock of sheep into wooden frames, and exploded a bomb, spreading spores of the deadly disease. Within three days the sheep started to die. Subsequent attempts to disinfect the island were unsuccessful, leading experts to conclude that 100 kg of anthrax spores dropped over a city could kill three million people, and leave it uninhabitable 'for genera-tions'. Eventually, in 1986, a major decontamination project took place, in which the entire island was soaked in formaldehyde and sea water, and in 1990, after extensive testing, the quarantine on the island was lifted.

1946
SCOTLAND'S SECOND NATIONAL DRINK

A.G. Barr & Co. were obliged by new legislation on the labelling of food and drink to change the name of their best-selling soft drink, hitherto called Strachan's Brew. But as Strachan's Brew was not brewed, it could no longer be called a brew. So Strachan's Brew was reincarnated as Irn Bru, the mangled spelling getting round the difficulty. Only two people in the company know the recipe, which is kept in a bank vault. And these two people are never allowed to fly in the same aeroplane. The only iron in Irn Bru is the 0.0002 per cent ferric nitrate listed in the ingredients.

1951

HER GRACE BESTOWS HER FAVOURS

Ian Douglas Campbell, 11th Duke of Argyll, married Margaret Whigham, the US-raised daughter of a Scottish millionaire. Celebrated for her good looks, Margaret lost her virginity at the age of 15 to the actor David Niven. She went on to become Debutante of the Year in 1930, before her first marriage in 1933. Before, during and after this first marriage (which ended in 1947) Margaret acquired a reputation for sexual voraciousness, and her friends noted that her appetites in this department increased markedly after she fell 40 feet down a lift shaft while visiting her chiropodist in 1943. Her watchword was, 'Go to bed early and often.'

Margaret's marriage to the Duke was not a happy one. He had a taste for the bottle, she for other men. In 1963 he hired a locksmith to break into a locked cupboard in her flat in Mayfair, where he discovered extensive evidence of her infidelities, which he later put before a court during his action for divorce. Among the evidence was a Polaroid photograph of the Duchess in her three-strand pearl necklace fellating a naked man, whose head was not visible. The identity of the Headless Man kept the tabloid press busy for many years, favoured candidates including Duncan Sandys, Minister of Defence at the time, and the film star Douglas Fairbanks Junior. After her divorce, the Duchess fell into debt. She died in penury in 1993.

1954

COW BEHAVES LIKE A BULL IN A CHINA SHOP

In Inverness a cow escaped a livestock auction, ran down the street and into a doorway. Mounting the stairs, it then fell through the floor into the shop below, where it ran amok. In the course of its rampage, it managed to turn on a tap, resulting in a flood. The owner of the shop sued the auction firm, but the judge ruled against the plaintiff, explaining that 'a gate-crashing, stair-climbing, floor-bursting, tap-turning cow was something *sui generis* [a unique case] for whose depredations the law affords no remedy unless there was foreknowledge of some such propensities'.

CHILDREN IN GORBALS HUNT VAMPIRE
WITH IRON TEETH

(23 September) To the amazement of their elders, hundreds of primary school children flocked to the Southern Necropolis, next door to the Gorbals in Glasgow. A rumour had spread like wildfire that haunting the cemetery was a seven-foot-high vampire with iron teeth who had killed and eaten two small boys. All evening, to a background of smoke and flares from the nearby steelworks, the children milled about, some of them carrying stakes (a necessary implement for dispatching vampires). The children returned to the Necropolis on two successive evenings, and their mass hysteria was matched by those of many grown-ups, who blamed imported American horror comics. The campaign against the latter, led by Gorbals MP Alice Cullen, eventually reached Westminster, and the result was the 1955 Children and Young Persons (Harmful Publications) Act. What the campaigners had failed to notice was that the Book of Daniel in the Bible contains a similar – perhaps even more terrifying – creature:

> After this I saw in the night visions, and behold a fourth beast, dreadful and terrible, and strong exceedingly; and it had great iron teeth: it devoured and brake in pieces, and stamped the residue with the feet of it: and it was diverse from all the beasts that were before it; and it had ten horns.

1955
SMALL ROCK ANNEXED TO THE CROWN

(18 September) A Royal Navy party from HMS *Vidal* was landed by helicopter on Rockall, a remote rock 240 miles to the west of Harris, and annexed it to the Crown. It appears the MoD wanted to prevent any hostile power from installing spying equipment on the rock, which lay in the path of missiles being test-fired from South Uist. Although the Soviet Union kept its own counsel, the same could not be said of J. Abrach Mackay, an 84-year-old local councillor, who on 7 November 1955 issued a strongly worded objection. 'My old father, God rest his soul, claimed that island for the Clan of Mackay in 1846,' he protested, 'and I now demand that the Admiralty hand it back. It's no' theirs.'

Mr Mackay's objection was brushed aside, and in 1972 the Island of Rockall Act formally incorporated the islet into the UK, specifically into 'that part known as Scotland'. As interest built in the fishing rights thereabouts, and more crucially in the potential for oil and gas extraction, other countries – Ireland, Iceland and Denmark – questioned whether an uninhabitable rock could be any nation's sovereign territory. To prove that it *was* habitable, in 1985 ex-SAS man Tom Maclean lived on the rock from 26 May to 4 July. In 1997 a small party of Greenpeace activists took up temporary residence as a protest against oil exploration in the area, and declared the islet to be the sovereign territory of Waveland.

1957
TREES FELLED TO ALLOW SPACESHIP TO LAND

Peter Caddy, a Harrow-educated member of the Rosicrucian Order Crotona Fellowship and a former officer in the catering branch of the RAF, together with his wife Eileen, took over the management of the Cluny Hill Hotel near Forres. It was the height of the Cold War, and the Caddys (according to Peter's autobiography *Perfect Time*) opened up discussions with extraterrestrials in order to negotiate an evacuation in case of nuclear apocalypse. The extraterrestrials were prepared to cooperate, and in 1961 they instructed the Caddys to fell an area of trees behind the hotel so that they could land their spaceship safely. The Caddys followed orders, but had failed to obtain the permission of the hotel's owner. This led to their dismissal. The following year, prompted by Eileen's 'inner voice', they moved into a caravan at Findhorn and were joined by their friend Dorothy Maclean. They started to grow vegetables, and attributed their success in this line of work to Dorothy's ability to communicate with plants. This claim attracted attention from a wide range of New Agers, and led to the establishment of the Findhorn Foundation.

The local villagers sometimes look askance at their neighbours. After going to a concert put on by the Foundation, the wife of the local pub landlord expressed her unhappiness with the proceedings. 'At the end they asked you to hug the people on either side of you,' she complained. 'It's not our way.' Peter Caddy was killed in a car crash in 1994. Eileen died in 2006.

1963

THE KNICKERBOCKER POLITICIAN AND THE ANTI-PANTIES PARTY

Death of Guy Alfred Aldred, an anarcho-communist known as the Knickerbocker Politician owing to his preferred mode of dress (to which were added an Eton collar, a starched shirt front, a black bow tie and a Norfolk jacket). Aldred was born in London in 1886, but moved to Glasgow after the First World War, where he stood in many elections for the Anti-Parliamentary Communist Federation – the so-called Anti-Panties. True to his principals, he urged people not to vote for him. By and large they took his advice.

1964

WHO'S COUNTING?

Forfar FC beat East Fife five–four. Fans are still awaiting the dream result: East Fife five, Forfar four.

1969

A LITTLE BIT OF THE HEBRIDES GOES TO THE MOON

(20 July) The first men landed on the Moon. With them they carried notepads fireproofed with alginate – a material made from seaweed harvested on Lewis.

1972

JUDGE REQUESTS TO BE TRAMPLED UPON BY GIRLS IN STILETTOS

On a visit to Troon in his role as Chief Reporter to Public Inquiries, Judge David Anderson was charged with approaching two 14-year-old girls in nearby Prestwick and asking them to go to a quiet place with him, where they were to walk over his naked body and subject him to a beating. His defence pointed out that a member of staff at the hotel where he was staying testified that his Bentley had not moved all night, and furthermore that the girls had failed to identify Anderson.

In addition, Anderson's wife testified that the coat he was supposedly wearing on the night in question was at that time at the cleaners. Nevertheless, Anderson was found guilty of a breach of the peace, fined £50, and, after exhausting the appeals process, was in 1974 dismissed from his posts. He himself was adamant that he had been framed by the KGB, who, he claimed, had employed a double to impersonate him. This was in revenge, he said, for his role in northern Norway in 1945 in putting down a revolt by Soviet PoWs held by the German army, a revolt that the West feared might herald an attempted takeover of the country by Stalin. Anderson's attempts to clear his name were to no avail, and in 2005, ten years after his death, the Scottish Criminal Cases Review Commission ruled that his conviction should stand.

In 2010, Lady Judy Steel, wife of the Liberal politician David Steel, shone an additional light on the case, when she described in her autobiography how as a young student in Edinburgh in 1959 she had been accosted by a well-dressed man in a car, who had told her he was 'something high up at the university' and that he had a bet on with a female friend, a Wren, as to how much pain he could withstand. Would she accompany him to a local gym and walk over his body in stiletto heels? She declined, but agreed to his request that she say nothing to anyone about the matter. Many years later, as she watched John Hale's play, *The Case of David Anderson QC*, she realised with horror that the man who propositioned her must have been Anderson, who at the time had been a law lecturer at Edinburgh University. The man, she remembered, had worn a Glenalmond tie.

1973
THE MORRIS MEN OF DEESIDE

An incomer from south of the Border formed the Banchory Morris Men, the only group of its kind in Scotland. Some years later, facing an alarming decline in numbers, one of the founder members commented, 'There's a limit as to how far most Scotsmen are willing to go to make a fool of themselves.'

1977

THE DECLINE AND FALL OF MISS NOYCE'S HOUSE OF PLEASURE

Death of Dora Noyce, Edinburgh's most famous madam, whose establishment in the New Town's elegant Danube Street was supposedly patronised by large sections of the city's Establishment. She herself claimed that business was briskest during the annual General Assembly of the Church of Scotland. Dressed in twinset and pearls, she cultivated the persona of a respectable Morningside lady, referring to her brothel as 'a house of leisure and pleasure' and 'a YMCA with extras'. The police were generally tolerant, given the orderliness of her house, but would come calling every now and again. 'Business or pleasure, officers?' Miss Noyce would enquire at the door.

1982

A CLASH OF IDEOLOGIES

A banner flown by Scots fans at a football match between Scotland and the Soviet Union carried a slogan summarising the nation's approach to the Cold War: 'Alcoholism vs Communism'. The result of the match was a draw.

DUKES OF ARGYLL STILL APPARENTLY EMBARRASSED

The Glasgow-based publisher Wm. Collins launched *Massacre: The Story of Glencoe* by former *Sunday Times* Insight journalist Magnus Linklater. The Collins sales representative who called at Inveraray Castle, seat of the Duke of Argyll, was told that the castle's shop would not be stocking the book. Three hundred years before, Archibald Campbell, 10th Earl (and later 1st Duke) of Argyll, had been colonel-in-chief of the regiment that undertook the massacre. The 10th Earl was also remembered for the conduct of his personal affairs. He was, according to George Lockhart (1673–1731), 'addicted to a lewd and profligate life'. He died in 1703 after being fatally stabbed during a brawl in a brothel.

GOD WILL HAVE TO PUNISH THE CITY OF GLASGOW, SAYS PASTOR

Among the candidates in the Glasgow Hillhead by-election was Pastor Jack Glass, standing for the 'Protestant Crusade Against the Papal Visit Party'. Glass gained only 388 votes, the victor being Roy Jenkins of the newly formed Social Democratic Party. Glass had denounced Jenkins as 'the Herod of Hillhead' – as Labour Home Secretary in the 1960s Jenkins had overseen the legalisation of abortion. Despite his poor showing, Glass successfully publicised his campaign against the visit to Glasgow of Pope John Paul II. As the Pope landed by helicopter in Bellahouston Park, Glass, together with his friend Dr Ian ('Save Ulster from Sodomy') Paisley and their massed acolytes uttered cries of 'The Beast Is Coming!', 'Down with the Pope of Rome!', 'Away with the Anti-Christ!' and so on. Glass and his followers then turned up on the Mound in Edinburgh to picket the popemobile as it drove past. The limousine slowed down as it passed by, so that John Paul could give Glass and his followers a blessing. It was said to be the only time that Glass was ever reduced to silence.

Glass had long been involved in an international campaign against Roman Catholicism and what he regarded as its undercover 'entry-ist' arm, the ecumenical movement. In 1966 he and Paisley travelled to Rome to picket the meeting of Dr Michael Ramsay, then Archbishop of Canterbury, and Pope Paul VI. They were detained for some hours by the Italian police, who thought their demonstration was something to do with the England football manager, Sir Alf Ramsey, who was then visiting Rome.

Glass mounted frequent protests against 'sacrilegious' shows and performers such as Marilyn Manson and Billy Connolly, describing the latter as a 'blasphemous buffoon' for his sketch transposing the Last Supper to the Saracen's Head in Glasgow's East End. 'If the Forth was lava,' Glass fulminated after a Connolly show in Edinburgh, 'I would throw him in.' In response, Connolly picketed Glass's church, holding a placard reading 'Jack is a Wee Pastor.'

When Glass was diagnosed with lung cancer, he asserted that it was a personal attack on him by Satan. 'The Devil would not pay much attention to me,' he said, 'if I wasn't doing something useful for God.' Shortly before his death in 2004 he announced that he didn't hate anyone, but, he insisted, 'Glasgow has turned its back on God. Sadly, God will have to punish it.' By this time even Dr Paisley had come to think of Glass as 'a bit of an extremist'.

1983

AN ERROR

Alasdair Gray's collection *Unlikely Stories, Mostly* contained an erratum stating: 'This slip has been inserted by mistake.'

ARTIST WINS BATTLE OF LITTLE SPARTA

The concrete poet and artist Ian Hamilton Finlay had begun creating his celebrated garden at Stonypath, Lanarkshire, in 1966, and had installed in it many works of art, largely classical in inspiration. In 1983 Strathclyde Regional Council informed him that they were increasing his rates, as the garden had been deemed to be an art gallery. On the contrary, Finlay argued, the garden was a temple and should therefore not be subjected to business rates. The Council sent in the bailiffs, but Finlay and his supporters successfully rebuffed the invasion in an encounter that became known as the Battle of Little Sparta.

1988

THATCHER PREACHES SERMON ON THE MOUND

In the Assembly Hall at the top of the Mound in Edinburgh, Prime Minister Margaret Thatcher addressed the General Assembly of the Church of Scotland. Amidst what Ludovic Kennedy described as 'a weird amalgam of fundamental Conservatism and simplistic Sunday school homilies', Thatcher asserted that Christianity, like free-market economics, was about choice, and that the social teaching of the Bible could be summed up in the phrase 'Create wealth.' Thatcher also quoted St Paul to the effect that 'If a man shall not work he shall not eat.' The Assembly members were aghast, and Thatcher's address became known as 'the Sermon on the Mound'.

1989

MP CHARGED WITH STEALING EX-MISTRESS'S KNICKERS

Ron Brown, the left-wing Labour MP for Leith, was charged with stealing two pairs of knickers from the flat of his former mistress. In the subsequent trial he was cleared of theft, but found guilty of causing criminal damage. Brown had been suspended from the House of Commons on several occasions, notably after damaging the Mace in 1988, which also led to a three-month withdrawal of the party whip. He was deselected prior to the 1992 election. Brown's Soviet sympathies prompted the KGB to make contact with him, with a view to cooperation. But the KGB decided it couldn't make use of him as an agent because they couldn't understand a word he said, so thick was his accent.

1991

THE SAD DEMISE OF BERNIE THE BULL

The causeway linking the small island of Vatersay to the larger island of Barra was opened to traffic. Prior to this, the farmers of Vatersay had been obliged to encourage their cattle to swim across the channel. In 1986 tragedy struck, when Bernie the prize bull drowned while trying to make the passage, perhaps having already exhausted himself carrying out his duties. Such was the outcry at his death that the government was obliged to act, and construction of the causeway began.

1993

NAVY DEFENDS ISLAND FROM MARAUDING SHEEP

The Orkney island of South Ronaldsay has a unique variety of sheep, one that subsists entirely on seaweed. The sheep are kept on the shore by a wall that runs right round the island, but this was badly damaged by storms in 1993. As the sheep burst through the gaps and rampaged across the fields, the Royal Navy was called in to fill up the breaches, if not with our English dead, then at least with some emergency fencing work.

1995

CRIMINAL CLASSES FIND INNOVATIVE USES FOR LAVATORY PAPER

A minor criminal called James Beattie raided a Kentucky Fried Chicken shop in Main Street, Rutherglen. Before committing the robbery, he had visited a public toilet and torn off yards of lavatory paper, which he wrapped round his head in an attempt to disguise himself. He then entered the shop and threatened the supervisor with a piece of broken glass, but fled when the till would not open. On 10 January 1996 Beattie was sentenced at the Glasgow High Court to 12 years in jail. The press dubbed him 'the Bog Roll Bandit'.

Another 'Bog Roll Bandit' hit the headlines in 2009, when at an identity parade a minor criminal called William Wingate attempted to disguise himself by shaving off his eyebrows and stuffing his cheeks with lavatory paper. Despite this, he was still identified as the man who had undertaken three raids on shops, armed with a knife, in the space of a fortnight. He was sentenced to eight years for robbery and attempting to pervert the course of justice.

BIRTH OF THE DEEP-FRIED MARS BAR

The first deep-fried Mars Bar is said to have been served in a chip shop in Stonehaven. Apparently the local schoolchildren would ask the proprietor to deep-fry a range of foods they brought in, and the deep-fried Mars Bar turned into an instant success. It was reported in the *Aberdeen Evening Express*, and then picked up by the nationals and the BBC, and within days deep-fried Mars Bars were on sale across the country – and became the epitome of the healthy Scottish diet.

1997

FINGERS POINT TO FAIRIES O' CARLOPS

The small village of Carlops, on the south side of the Pentland Hills, is celebrated among the scientific community as the birthplace of C. T. R. Wilson (1869–1959), winner of the 1927 Nobel Prize for Physics and inventor of the Wilson cloud chamber. However, the irrational will out. Not only does the village take its name from the Carlin's Loup ('witch's leap'), a sheer rock in the village from which a witch is said to have flown, but in more recent times, in 1997, a mobile telephone mast near to the village, to which the inhabitants had objected, mysteriously disappeared overnight. The locals were unanimously agreed that it was the 'Fairies o' Carlops' who were to blame.

TORTOISESHELL CAT MISTAKEN FOR BEAST OF BALMORAL

Reports of a black panther roaming the area round Balmoral Castle put the local gamekeepers onto high alert. One of them, believing he had the beast in his sights, let off a shot – and found that he had killed the tortoiseshell cat of the minister of Craithie Kirk, where the Queen worships while staying at her Highland residence.

2000

ANSWER TO A HEADLINE WRITER'S PRAYER

Caledonian Thistle's decisive victory over Celtic in the Scottish Cup supplied *The Sun* with the ultimate dream of all headline writers: 'Super Cally Go Ballistic, Celtic Are Atrocious'.

SCOTS STILL IN DANGER IN CITY OF YORK

It was still legal to kill a Scotsman within the city walls of York, but only if he was carrying a bow and arrow. There still supposedly exists a law in Scotland that if someone knocks on your door and asks to use your lavatory, you must allow them to do so (but whether this is actually a law or just traditional good manners is a little vague).

2003

THE MYSTERIOUS ISLAND OF TEN EN A

The *Bookseller* magazine reported the following conversation heard in an Edinburgh bookshop:

> *American customer:* Do you have a map of Ten en a?
> *Bookseller:* Ten en a, sir? Where is that?
> *American customer:* Well, it's a little island off the west coast of Scotland [IONA].

POTENTIAL FOR WMD DETECTED IN INNER HEBRIDES

As US and UK forces prepared to inflict shock and awe on the people of Iraq, operatives at the US Defense Threat Reduction Agency, while surfing the Web, identified the Bruichladdich distillery on the island of Islay as a potentially lethal threat to world peace. Apparently, with 'just a small tweak', its facilities could be converted to the production of chemical weapons. The natives of Islay girded themselves for the expected onslaught.

MAN WALKS LENGTH OF LOCH NESS UNDERWATER

Lloyd Scott spent 12 days walking along the bottom of Loch Ness kitted out in an old-fashioned diver's suit, with lead boots and round metal helmet fed with air via a tube from the surface. In total his kit weighed 120 lb, and the 26 miles he walked was the equivalent of a marathon. He said the experience had been 'cold and lonely', but worth it: he was raising money for children with leukaemia.

2007

DEMISE OF THE MUCH HONOURED THE LAIRD OF BLADNOCH AND LOCHANBARDS

Scotland lost one of its more colourful incomers with the death of His Excellency Colonel Professor Chevalier Helmut Bräundle-Falkensee GCJ, FMA, MEASc, Grand Master of the Order of St Joachim and The Much Honoured the Laird of Bladnoch and Lochanbards. Needless to say His Excellency had a passion for heraldry.

2008

A NEW DANGER: DOOKING FOR APPLES

The traditional Halloween custom of dooking for apples, in which the contestants plunge their heads into a tub of water and attempt to retrieve apples with their teeth, was banned in many primary schools on the grounds of hygiene. The following year one head teacher gave another reason: 'It's too big a temptation for the staff just to hold some of the kids' heads under until they drown.'

2009

BUCKFAST KORMA

The *Hamilton Advertiser* reported that the local House of Shah takeaway was offering a new dish, Buckfast Korma. Although brewed by monks in Devon, Buckfast Tonic Wine has become particularly popular in the Glasgow area, where it goes by a number of nicknames, including Electric Soup, Commotion Lotion and Wreck-the-Hoose Juice, all alluding to its tendency to increase the aggression of the imbiber. Cal Shah, the proprietor of House of Shah, told the *Advertiser*, 'I always noticed that Buckfast was something that certain people like to drink, and because it was so popular within the local area I added it to the ingredients. Some of my customers have even asked for Buckie Bhoona.' Mr Shah previously owned a takeaway in Motherwell, where one of the dishes on offer was Chicken Lager Tikka.

2012

ARMSTRONG THE GOOD GIRAFFE

A man called Armstrong Baillie hit the headlines after making public appearances as 'Armstrong the Good Giraffe'. Twice a week Armstrong, an unemployed man from Dundee, would don a giraffe costume (including long neck) made for him by his mother and travel to different parts of Scotland to commit good deeds, such as handing out bananas to runners in the Edinburgh half marathon, clearing litter off Portobello beach, cleaning out cages in cat homes, handing out £10 vouchers to mothers in hospitals, and presenting passers-by with cups of coffee on cold mornings. He funded his acts of charity with the cash he raised by busking with his kazoo and djembe drum, and saved money by hitch-hiking to his destinations. Unfortunately, the length of his neck meant that he was only able to accept lifts from open-topped convertibles. 'Giraffes are like me,' he said, 'as my head is in the clouds but my heart is in the right place.' Mostly he received a good welcome from people, but once a Kevin Bridges [a Scottish stand-up comedian] lookalike tried to pull his head off in a pub. 'It might have been the real Kevin Bridges,' Baillie mused, 'as I didn't have my glasses on.' He got a mixed reaction from dogs, and was once chased by a beagle.

MAN DRESSED AS PENGUIN WINS MORE VOTES THAN LIB DEMS

(May) A candidate styling himself Professor Pongoo (in reality Mike Ferrigan, a climate activist) won more first-preference votes than the Liberal Democrats in Pentland Hills, one of Edinburgh City Council's wards. Lib Dems and Labour, said Professor Pongoo, may 'talk the talk', but, he said, 'as a penguin I can show them how to walk the walk'.

A UFO OVER BAILLIESTON

(2 December) The pilot and co-pilot of an Airbus A320 approaching Glasgow Airport reported that while flying about 1,200 metres above the Baillieston area of Glasgow they had seen an object 'loom ahead' of them, about 100 metres away. The object, which appeared to be

blue and yellow in colour and 'bigger than a balloon', passed directly underneath the Airbus. It did not show up on the radar of air-traffic control. The incident was reported as a near miss, but investigators were unable to say what the unidentified flying object might have been, having ruled out gliders, hangliders, microlights, weather balloons, and all other known possibilities.

2014
MESSAGES OF DEFIANCE

A Glasgow motorist, disgruntled that his battered old runabout had been wheel-clamped, left a message for the clampers scrawled along the side of the vehicle: 'Fucking keep it.'

Meanwhile, in Edinburgh, a chip shop was closed down by health inspectors, a notice affixed to the window explaining that this was due to an infestation of mice. An irate customer stuck up his own notice next to the official one. 'Whae geez a fuck aboot mice!???' the notice said. 'I dinnae go tae a chippy tae get healthy, YA C*NTS!'

2015
WE STILL KNOW OUR PLACE

(January) The Earl of Hopetoun, who lives in a vast stately home near Edinburgh, advertised on Gumtree for a live-in help to carry out such tasks as ironing shirts, polishing silver, and carrying heavy suitcases and vases. The advertisement said the position would suit a recent graduate, and that the successful candidate would be expected to remain in post for at least three years. Accommodation, but not food, was offered. There was no mention of a salary.

Index